THE PERFECT DAY

40 YEARS OF *SURFER* MAGAZINE

EDITED BY SAM GEORGE

CHRONICLE BOOKS
SAN FRANCISCO

Library of Congress Cataloging-in-Publication-Data

The perfect day : 40 years of Surfer magazine / edited by Sam George.

    168p.   25.5 x 30.5 cm.

    ISBN 0-8118-3117-5

    1. Surfing. I. Surfer.

GV840.S8 P42 2000

    797.3'2—dc21   00-057098

Printed in Hong Kong

Casewrap photo: David Puu

Page 3 photo: Bernard Testamale

BOOK DESIGN - *SAMUELS DARNALL & ASSOCIATES*

ART DIRECTOR - *REGINA FRANK*

PHOTO EDITOR - *JEFF DIVINE*

PROJECT DIRECTOR - *SEAN SMITH*

PROJECT MANAGER - *EVELYN TURNER*

Distributed in Canada by Raincoast Books
9050 Shaughnessy Street
Vancouver, British Columbia V6P 6E5

10 9 8 7 6 5 4 3 2 1

Chronicle Books LLC
85 Second Street
San Francisco, California 94105

www.chroniclebooks.com

FOREWORD

BY MATT WARSHAW

In 18 months, my editor at Harcourt Brace hopes to see a completed first-draft manuscript for a reference book titled *The Encyclopedia of Surfing*. Word count: 500,000. A nice, round, surreal figure. Just tapping it out brings a small tremor of anxiety. I therefore spent the opening months of 2000 entering the first four decades of SURFER magazine into a Filemaker Pro database, volumes 1 through 40 inclusive, 360 issues, 1960 to 1999, searchable by topic, article title, author, date, issue number, and cover subject. A research aid for the still-incubating *Encyclopedia*. A stall tactic for the same. The latest and most extravagant display of an obsessive-compulsive affliction that won't always submit to yoga and candle-lit aromatherapy baths. All of the above; a massive, multipurpose job. But the thing's finished for the moment (yearly updates to come), and I can now maneuver with astonishing ease across the length and breadth of SURFER's oceanic data field: Five Summer Stories debuts at the Santa Monica Civic Auditorium (July issue, 1972). George Downing beats Rabbit Kekai for the Makaha title (spring 1962) after a 10-week mid-event postponement—weeks, not days—due to flat surf. The Eagles' "Hotel California" tops a readers poll of Top Ten Songs to Surf By (July 1977), followed by Linda Ronstadt's "Heat Wave" and Neil Young's "Cowgirl in the Sand." No mention of sample size or statistical methodology, but Ronstadt's inclusion raises questions. Eulogies for Duke Kahanamoku, Snowy McAlister, and Dewey Weber (May 1968, April 1989 and May 1993, respectively). Todd Chesser says that "big-wave danger is minimal" (December 1994), and is eulogized himself two and a half years later (June 1997) after drowning in big surf. Ninety percent of respondents to a 1999 readers survey are male (February 1999), 73 percent are under 30, and 63 percent are regularfoot. Tom Curren is preferred to Kelly Slater, 54 percent to 46 percent. Santa Barbara surfers cross-hatch 282 boards to the roof of a Humvee (also in February 1999), drive the requisite 100 feet without losing any cargo, and thus *double* the old board-stacking record of 141.

Nothing too profound here—death notices aside. But each reference has, I think, a kind of spark; each seems to catch and reflect the light of an activity that has always burned well past the boundaries of sport and recreation. "It's all surfing," as barefoot inventor Tom Morey told SURFER in 1994.

"Everything! Surfing in the ocean just happens to be the purest form of surfing." Downing's long-delayed win at the Makaha contest, at some level, speaks to this kind of intensity. Board-stacking, too. If such items are trivial, to me they're trivial and wonderful at the same time. Most people, surfers included, won't experience the same hit of satisfaction I get from being able to arrange the following hierarchical listing of pre-2000 SURFER cover subjects: Kelly Slater (the record holder at 11 covers), Tom Curren (9), the Ho brothers, Derek and Michael (9 combined), Gerry Lopez (5), Mark Richards (4), Shaun Tomson (3), Bill Hamilton (2), Brian Hamilton (*Brian* Hamilton?) (2), Narrabeen's Col Smith (1), San Diego's Col Smith (1), Newcastle's Col Smith (0), and Mickey Dora (0). Yes, indeed, this may be real insider-only stuff. Not for dabblers. It's an arbitrary line, I realize, between the merely arcane and the genuinely tedious, but SURFER, by any definition, has with some regularity published items that glaze the eyes of even the most fervid and detail-obsessed reader: results for *all 28 separate divisions* of an NSSA National Championships contest, for example, or another stage-managed Indonesia boat trip, or the latest post-Thruster board-design guru's sagacious comment about this year's model being a "refinement" on last year's.

But just about anybody, I believe, surfer or nonsurfer, can appreciate that this rich, intricate, joyous sport has, for 40 years without a break, been so neatly gathered and ordered under the SURFER banner. Forty years—a great accomplishment by publishing standards. A wonderful gift to surfing. SURFER'S hoary "Bible of the Sport" designation has always left me cold, in part because it doesn't seem broad enough. Better, I think, that the magazine be viewed and honored as surfing's great yearbook and archive, forum and marketplace, gallery and parade ground.

As publisher-in-training John Severson pieced together the 36-page debut issue of THE SURFER in the spring of 1960, doing layout work in the living room of his Dana Point apartment in Southern California while his wife, Louise, proofed and retyped articles in the bedroom-office, he made a conscious decision—a philosophical decision, in fact—to present surfing as happily self-exiled from the world of sport. "We were a little removed from society in general," Severson told me in 1994. "That's what held us together as

PHOTO: DAVID PUU

surfers. And I think to some degree that's what held the magazine together as well." Severson distilled this idea into surfing's most graceful aphorism, printed originally as the editorial sign-off to the first issue, beneath a photo of an anonymous surfer knee-paddling toward an empty lineup. "In this crowded world," he wrote, "the surfer can still seek and find the perfect day, the perfect wave, and be alone with the surf and his thoughts." Surf contests, surf business, surf glory, even in 1960, were there for the taking. And surfing, moreover, for lack of a more suitable category, *is* a sport. But Severson's "perfect day, perfect wave" adage gave surfing a kind of permanent aesthetic address. No cheering spectators. No end zones or playoffs, and nothing to win except peace of mind.

SURFER began as a photo book (just two articles appeared in the first issue: a how-to piece and a short fiction essay), and the magazine might today be viewed as primarily an exhibit hall for Ron Stoner, Art Brewer, Jeff Divine, Warren Bolster, Don King, and dozens of other talented masthead photographers of the past four decades. The best are celebrated, even venerated, within the surf world. Their work spins away from the confines of surf publishing altogether and turns up on billboards, or in the feature pages of *Life*, *National Geographic*, and *Sports Illustrated*, or in art books of size, weight, and glossiness commensurate with those on Picasso or Warhol.

But if SURFER takes much of its shape and structure from photographs, it is animated by the voices, thoughts, and opinions of its writers. The second issue of SURFER was positively bulging with articles compared to the first, with three features, a fiction piece, and an editorial; and from that point on, the magazine became surfing's first and best repository of letters. There's been much to communicate—including the importance of communication itself. "Surfing," as editor Drew Kampion wrote in 1970, "is the medium through which we must speak to each other. Later we may find we share a love of nature, a desire for peace, a need for love, a common friend, or a particular belief. But first, because this is a surfing magazine . . . first we have surfing." (And before judging Kampion to be overly solemn and pontifical, keep in mind that he penned SURFER's "First Annual End of the World Issue!" cover blurb in 1970, and wrote a commentary on the 1980 presidential election

surf-off at Cotton's Point between Richard Nixon, George "Whitewater" Wallace, and Mickey Dora. With Dora, naturally, coming out on top.)

Because I am a former SURFER editor, my appraisal of the magazine's literary worth could well be biased to the point of worthlessness. Or forget the editorship, I'm a 31-year subscriber. So of course I'm biased. Even so, I present as an article of objective truth the idea that SURFER, year in and year out, has outclassed the competition mainly because of its writers. Tap into the database to find something of pith and substance on a given surf topic—localism, surf camps, Lisa Andersen, the '66 world titles, big waves, Maverick's, twin-fins—and chances are the definitive work is in a SURFER back issue, written (probably) by Kampion, John Witzig, Phil Jarratt, Bruce Valluzzi, Matt George, Sam George, Derek Hynd, Steve Barilotti, Dave Parmenter, Ben Marcus, Bruce Jenkins, or Steve Hawk.

Yes, banal text is also produced with regularity. Banal or worse. Giving famous surfers writing assignments, for one thing, usually makes about as much sense as giving ASP wildcard entries to surf journalists. But let it go. SURFER was and remains the sport's brightest, nimblest, most articulate voice, on matters ranging from near-atomic particularity—identifying the base composition of wax, for example, in "Sticky Business: A Survey of Surf Wax"—all the way up to the pursuit of a unifying surf theory, in cover stories such as "Why We Surf" and "What Is Surfing?"

John Severson himself wrote the introduction for "What Is Surfing?" in 1970, just before he sold the magazine and moved to Hawaii. At one point he goes for austerity. Surfing, he says, is "man simply riding a plastic surfboard on waves." But elsewhere he braids surfing to music, dance, sport, and nothing less than the "indwelling nature of God." In summary he offers a benediction for all nonaggressive points of view, and does so with a smile. "Surfing is whatever we think it is—and always fun." Neatly done. Severson answers the question on the essential nature of surfing and leaves a mission statement, graciously adhered to for the most part, for SURFER editors and publishers to come.

Simple and complex by turns. Always fun.

What's true for surfing is true as well for its best magazine.

INTRODUCTION

BY SAM GEORGE

The inspiration to put together *The Perfect Day: 40 Years of SURFER Magazine* is rooted in a motivation as old as surfing itself. By its very nature, surfing is an anticipatory sport: the next swell, the next wave, the next ride might be the best ever. Surfers live with this constant state of anticipation—of agitation, if you will—in all manner of devotion. Some drop off the charts completely, sacrificing everything that binds them to common society—career, family, possessions—so that they may share the ocean's heartbeat and never miss another good wave. Others reconcile themselves to the estrangement, fall out of rhythm, surrendering their zeal to creeping nostalgia, dreams of warm, sunny days, trusty boards, and swells long past. But for the rest, there has been SURFER Magazine. Forty years of it, each issue looked forward to with as much inspired anticipation as the swells that have rolled through its pages. First 6 times a year, then 12, but for all those years—for all those eras—the only waves a surfer could truly count on, the only waves you could hold in your hand. It's only natural, then, that we should want to collect the very best of those years and bind them into one volume. All the surfers, all the waves, all the color, travel, humor, the ideas and dreams of three generations of barefoot adventurers splashing onto the page and then spilling off like sea spray. To be read, enjoyed, and then put aside, the measure of a surfer's memories. Because at the dawn of this new century of surfing, as in the century past, only one thing is certain: There will be another wave. And this one could be the best ever.

For these 40 years of stoke, we'd like to acknowledge the former editors of SURFER, each contributing his vision to the magazine's timeline, each individual voice the essence of the *The Perfect Day*:

JOHN SEVERSON—1960–65
PATRICK MCNULTY—1965–68
DREW KAMPION—1968–71
STEVE PEZMAN—1971–79
JIM KEMPTON—1979–82
PAUL HOLMES—1982–90
MATT WARSHAW—1990–91
STEVE HAWK—1991–99
EVAN SLATER—1999–00

JOHN SEVERSON
PHOTO: ART BREWER

In this crowded world the surfer can still seek and find the perfect day, the perfect wave, and be alone with the surf and his thoughts . . .

— JOHN SEVERSON

Chapter One

The Sixties
This Is Revolution

The story of SURFER Magazine is not unlike most others worth listening to: it's all about love. Love of a sport, yes, but of so much more. The surfing way of life has always demanded of its faithful something more akin to pure devotion than the simple dedication that characterizes mere sport. In the spring of 1960, John Severson, a 26-year-old art teacher, graphic designer and surf filmmaker from San Clemente, California, gave this passion a face, a voice and a name: a relatively crude 36-page, black-and-white, hand-illustrated magazine called *The Surfer*.

Surfers in the early 1960s were a tribe yearning to be united. The earliest surf films, seminal imagery that fired so many imaginations throughout the 1950s, brought surfers together, yet hardly defined them or the lifestyle they were in the midst of creating. These 16mm moments flickering on the screens of beach-city high school auditoriums were too fleeting, too ephemeral, to galvanize a generation. Surfers needed something they could hold in their hands, a banner under which they could make their barefoot stand against the conformity of the age. And this, for the very first time, is what *The Surfer* gave them.

Originally an accompanying piece for *Surf Fever*, Severson's then-latest surf film, *The Surfer*, launched as a "one-off," with 10,000 copies to be hand-distributed out of a Volkswagen van along the coast of Southern California. Severson sold approximately half his issues. But when he took *The Surfer* quarterly in 1961, the response was immediate and enthusiastic. The entire pressrun of 5,000 sold out in only three months. Surfing's voice—its authority—was born.

The Surfer of the early 1960s gathered its pace. A pattern of content was set that would hold true for most of the decade, the message being, essentially, "Hey, look what's going on here. Isn't this bitchin'?" Severson was assembling the tribes, with travel features like "Santa Cruz: Northern Outpost" (Vol. 2, No. 1), "Peru: Las Olas Grandes" (Vol. 2, No. 2) and "The Australian Surf" (Vol. 2, No. 3) reeling in the disparate corners of surfing's watery globe.

Surfing competitions were reported on, and fiction, mostly of a whimsical nature, was featured, as was artwork by Severson, Rick Griffin, Mike Salisbury and John Van Hamersveld.

Editorially, innovation and irreverence rode alongside an odd measure of conservatism. With its name shortened simply to SURFER in 1964, and its publication increased to bimonthly issues, the magazine broke new ground graphically, its look predating many of the trends that would later come to characterize the Swinging Sixties. Use of Day-Glo logos, split-image covers and deceptively pre-psychedelic subversive artwork from Griffin, combined with technically advanced color action photography and a prescient vision of adventure travel, gave the SURFER of the mid-1960s a cutting-edge flair. Photographers like the incomparable Ron Stoner mirrored in their lenses the bright spectrum of surfing's rainbow, while writers like Bill Cleary and Craig Lockwood added eloquence to "awhoooo!" Yet this slick, vibrant package often gilded a surprisingly "straight" message from editor Severson, who once spoke out against what he perceived as a growing trend of hooliganism ("The real surfers are disgusted and have reached the end of their patience. It's the start of a new era in surfing—or it's the end of surfing!"), and later from former AP reporter Patrick McNulty, who during his 1964–67 editorial tenure at SURFER railed in his monthly column against everything from pot smoking to long hair.

But by 1967, SURFER was riding a groundswell of counterculture, with the entire surfing world at the crest, and it was then that its readers—its followers—began shaping the magazine in their own image. In 1968, a young editor named Drew Kampion was hired to make sense of the changes that had inflamed a generation. He instead touched off an explosion of antiestablishment free expression that rocked surfing to its core. While the rest of the country was still "talkin' 'bout a revolution," the surfers' magazine already had it in print. SURFER in the 1960s took surfing journalism from Genesis to New Testament in 10 short years.

THE SURFER BI-MONTHLY

A John Severson Production

75¢

RM aff

VOL. 3 NO. 3   AUG. – SEPT.

THE INTERNATIONAL SURFING MAGAZINE

MORE OF MURPHY

BERNARD "MIDGET" FARRELLY
1964 WORLD CONTEST
PHOTO: RON PERROTT

Volume 2 | Number 3

WHAT IS "THE SURFER"?

It is with a great deal of pleasure that we announce the quarterly publication of THE SURFER. Each spring, summer, fall and winter edition will bring you the tops in surf photography and accurate surf coverage. John Severson will photograph and illustrate THE SURFER and will bring you informative articles on the surfing world.

John Severson first attempted to pick up a surfboard in 1946. It weighed 125 lbs., and he couldn't. A year later he purchased a lightweight (80 lb.) hollow board and launched his surfing career. A year later he stood up. His subsequent rise in the surfing world has been equally as spectacular as his first year. In the winter of 1957–58 he was seen frequently in the big surf and was present on the "big day," January 13, 1958, when Makaha reached the preposterous size of thirty feet. While taking the drop on one of the biggest waves of the day, John was "planted" by the wave and fortunate to escape with his life. It was in 1957 that John began to turn his hobby of photography toward surfing films, producing *Surf Safari* and *Surf Fever*.

John still rides the big surf whenever possible. In February of this year he won the International Surfing Contest held in Peru at Kon Tiki Beach. He also set a new record in the 5-mile open sea paddle, battering Rabbit Kekai's mark by one minute. Severson's knowledge of the surf, its history, and the people, along with his background in journalism, art, music and education, help bring you the best in surf movies and surf magazines.

Master surfer Phil Edwards, asked by SURFER to examine various competitive approaches, instead provided a definition of style that is as valid today as it was in 1964.

Volume 5 | *Number 1*
WHAT IS GOOD?

BY PHIL EDWARDS

In contest surfing, there are two schools of thought. There is the "stylist." I have been termed this by many people who have borrowed the word from skiing. As far as I can ascertain, applied to surfing, it would mean that the surfer concentrates primarily on maintaining complete control at all times—with good form (whatever that is). This naturally limits maneuverability and tricks.

I know of no name for the other school or style, but in every surfing contest I have judged, there was always the contestant who "gets the job done." These surfers do many things on a board and are willing to lose some control and composure and even take an occasional spill. In contrast, there will be an equally good surfer doing a little bit less, but always maintaining control. In other words, the "stylist" will look smoother, but he won't be doing as much. If he was, he wouldn't look as smooth, and vice versa.

Remember, there are two schools of thought—often it becomes apparent in the style. In the first, the wave is an incidental means of expressing one's ability to others; often a gym or track field would serve the same purpose. In the second, or other school, a wave is simply a beautiful expression of nature and respected as reason enough to participate. The "stylist" merges with the wave, while the former merely "uses" the wave.

What is good?

For the first time ever, the "best surfer in the world" was chosen by SURFER readers.

Volume 5 | Number 3

SURFER POLL

BY HEVS McCLELLAND

"Tonight we're going to recognize these men according to a poll . . . in which literally thousands of readers have responded. And when you see the 20 men who gather behind me on the speaker's platform, you'll finally shake your head and you may change the order a little bit in your own minds, but you'll say, 'By golly, there are some fantastic surfers up there.' This is what we're offering here tonight—the first of its kind—the response to who are the best surfers in the world in terms of A) surfing skill, B) contribution to the sport, and C) their knowledge of the sea and how well-known they are by other surfers."

PHIL EDWARDS
*1964 SURFER POLL WINNER (LEFT),
WITH HEVS McCLELLAND*
PHOTO: SURFER ARCHIVES

DUKE KAHANAMOKU
PHOTO: RON STONER

The legendary Duke Kahanamoku, Olympic star, Hawaiian ambassador and surfing's lion in winter, "talked story."

Volume 6 | Number 1

THE DUKE

CAN YOU TELL US ABOUT ONE OF YOUR BIGGEST RIDES ON A SURFBOARD?

Yes, I can say that, too. One was really fantastic. I caught this big wave—I would say between 25 and 30 feet, on one of those days when the surf was so big. Well, a lot of the guys just grounded themselves, and the others were still surfing, and I picked up this 16-foot board of mine and went to Castles. And I looked at those doggone waves and I said, "Boy, these are really top waves," and I said, "I'm going to take it whether I like it or not." I had to go. [Laughing] And I caught this wave and I came in. I started from Castles right out through Queen's Surf; that's Queen's Surf on the other side, close to the Canoes Surf. That's where I toppled. The point of my board hit the edge and knocked my balance. That was the end of my run. Otherwise, if I hadn't done that, I would have gone right to Harry Steiner's Waikiki Tavern. I could have gone all the way in [to the beach]. The ride was about a mile and one eighth. Yeah, about a mile and one eighth, and that's a long stretch.

KEMP AABERG
EYES EMPTY RINCON
PHOTO: RON STONER

Laguna Beach surfboard builder Fred Wardy, known for his quirky, literate advertisements, penned this passionate manifesto for a SURFER photo feature.

Volume 6 | *Number 1*

SURFING IS

BY FRED WARDY

Surfing is many things to many individuals, but, purely and simply, a healthy, vigorous, beautiful sport. Surfing is a release from exploding tensions of 20th-century living, escape from the hustling, bustling city world of steel and concrete, a return to nature's reality.

For sheer spontaneous action, surfing is unbeatable. It quenches man's thirst for challenging natural elements. Spiritually and physically, it makes the surfer part of the sea, while the sea, in turn, becomes part of him.

Surfing is excitement and physical diversion, yet more. Like all great sports, surfing is a succession of experiences, sensations and impressions . . . a remembrance of lazy days at a favorite beach, laughter, friendship, golden sunsets and fires at dusk.

Surfing is climbing from a warm bed in predawn's coolness, a sleepy drive, coffee and doughnuts at a roadside diner and the clatter of surfboards as they're unstacked from a car rack. Surfing is the joy of watching a sun rise slowly into the sky. It's crisp, clean waves, crests blown high by an offshore wind. It's gray mist, dampness and cold sand under bare feet, the lonely cry of a gull sweeping across silent, brooding seas. On a big day, surfing is a strong swell and waves that have lost their playfulness. Then it's stomach knots, high exultation, a trace of fear.

Surfing is sharing a wordless silence, broken only by the sound of a bar of wax moving back and forth across a board. It's mounting tension before the first takeoff, enthusiasm for the next wave when the ride is over.

Surfing is a good ride, brief seconds yet a culmination of endless hours on a board. These fleeting moments of exhilaration and release are days, months, years of time and experience.

Surfing is the endless search for a windless day, an uncrowded beach, the perfect wave.

Surfing is a special kind of madness, a feeling for the sea, a combination of love, knowledge, respect, fear—instinctive perception gained through repeated contact. Surfing is a moment of achievement, of glory, of unsung triumph. For the man, surfing is freedom and youth rediscovered, and for the boy, a means of expression vital to his being. For both, it's fun.

Surfing is great.

BILL FURY
STONER'S POINT, MEXICO
PHOTO: RON STONER

Associate editor Bill Cleary helped create surfing's enduring Myth of Perfection.

Volume 6 | Number 4

MEXICAN MALIBU

BY BILL CLEARY

"Ah yes, Señor, the wave climbs high until even the sun is lost behind it . . . we call it 'Ola Verde.'"

"Have you seen it?"

"But no, Señor. Still, I have heard many stories. . . ."

There have always been many myths of huge green waves, undiscovered spots, perfect breaks abounding in Mexico. But like the El Dorado sought by the ancient Spanish conquistadores, the treasure is always over the next hill, beyond the distant jungle.

As a frequent south-of-the-border surfer, I often had heard tales of undiscovered surfing paradises. Now there was a new myth—the story of a Mexican Malibu. Was it just another tall tale? Another wild Mexican goose chase? I had to find out, and so I was on the trail—tracking the myth to its source.

It was just before Easter, and I found myself deep in the forests of Beverly Hills, on the winding road that leads to the Bel Air Hotel and the bungalow of Peter Viertel—the man, I had heard, who held the key to the Myth.

In the hotel lobby, I picked up an antique phone. "Mr. Peter Viertel, please." A secretary with a pleasant English-scented voice gave directions, and moments later, I was in the bungalow and shaking hands with Viertel—the man with the Secret.

Viertel is a novelist, a screenwriter and—what most impressed me—a surfing pioneer. Several years ago while working on the screenplay of *The Sun Also Rises*, Viertel introduced surfing to France's Côte du Basque. He also had surfed Mexico while his wife, Deborah Kerr, was filming *The Night of the Iguana* at the picturesque village of Puerta Vallarta. There, I had been told, Viertel had discovered the Mexican Malibu.

In the bungalow, we talked as surfers: places we had surfed, about the crowds taking over the sport, of Viertel's place on the Spanish coast where (as yet) no one surfs—where the writer is alone with the waves.

I wanted to turn the conversation to Mexico, to the hidden Malibu, but how? I grew nervous and was just about to blurt my question when Viertel, perhaps intuitively, began speaking of Mexico and Puerta Vallarta. As I listened, he described a series of beautiful coves, points and reefs; lobsters crawling from the sea; warm, clear water and pink-sand beaches. He had seen a world of surf and he told no tales. I could barely contain my excitement.

"How does one get there?"

"By Jeep," Viertel said, "it's about three hours through the jungle. But Jeeps are expensive. I think it's easier by boat."

"But it's hard to recognize surfing spots from the water. Are there any landmarks? Is there a village nearby?"

"Here," he said, sitting down at a desk. "I'll draw you a map. . . ."

CLAUDE CODGEN
LIDO BEACH, LONG ISLAND, NY
PHOTO: RON STONER

The trend of hanging 10 was deemed "a sport within a sport."

Volume 6 | *Number 5*
NOSERIDING

"Even if Nuuhiwa didn't invent riding the nose while side-slipping through the soup, if he keeps it up . . . I'll give him credit for inventing it."
— *PHIL EDWARDS*

DAVID NUUHIWA
RULING ON THE NOSE
PHOTO: RON STONER

This humorous fiction piece, celebrating a surfing Christmas and the sport's Island roots, was cowritten by the Patterson brothers, a stylish trio of Hawaiian surfer/board builders.

Volume 6 | Number 6

DA KINE CHREESMESS FAIRSTORY

BY ROBERT, RAYMOND AND RONALD PATTERSON

Once upon one time get dis big fat bugga in one da kine red and white Lauhala, he like take plenty toy stuffs to all da keiki's aroun da worl'. Chee, dis bugga so fass he make 'em all ovah da place in jes one nite.

All ye-ah long he live in da snow by Califrisco somewhere, wid one whole bunch menehunes an dey make all kine toys like you nevah like beleve. Plenty ye-ahs was gone already, and dis bugga never went stop in Hawaii, 'cause no more chimilys on da house, an he like show how he can clime down chimilys, espeshly da hard kine.

One shocka day, dis small beachboy was bitin' hes toenails an he went say, "Mo bettah I go write dis bugga, all da haole guys come ovah an dey tell me dis guy went giv'm for Chreesmess." So he went write one letta to da Sandy Claws for get his okole ovah heah wid all da free toy stuffs.

Jes 'cause dis, watch you tink went happin da nex yeah? Wen Chreesmess went come aroun', da small boy went put hes head outside da window (he no comb hes hair you know), but he went spock dat Claws bugga way out on top da horizontals paddgeling for one big rave outsigh Public Bats. Da ting was way ovah hes head, too. He shoot 'em all da way thru Cunha's, smok 'em thru Queens, an no keedin' dis bugga had one big opu shakin jes like one bowl full poi. Hes face look like one ovah-ripe downside-up pineapple, an look like he nevah went shave for tree or even fo aloha weeks. On top hes head had one big red papale, an I never beleve wen I went see da big Lauhala bag on top hes bak stay full of plenny toy stuffs.

Wen da boy went see dis he went comb hes hair fass, brush hes teet wid Gleem, bite all hes dirty fingahnails off, an went run down for see Sandy Claws land on da beach.

Dis Claws was one shap surfer! He went cut bak an ride da curl tru Caone's and bye 'm bye went step right on da beach, an mo queeka den you can say "Duke Kahanamoku," he went put all da toy stuffs an bawds in front da Royal Hawaiian Hotel. Queek like one jax rabbits, he jump on hes bawd again an went paddle by Diamond Head for da horizontal. Even wen he was far away, we went hear him exscreem, "Merry Chreesmess to all you guys an Alohaaa!"

SANDY CLAWS
ART: RICK GRIFFIN

1965 was no summer of love at Malibu's annual club contest, where a clash of surfing titans turned ugly. Of note is SURFER's disclaimer: "As a judge, Bill Cleary had a ringside seat at the recent Malibu Contest. Cleary is not condoning the antics during the finals, and SURFER has taken a definite stand against them. However, it happened, and here's Cleary's description of THE DAY WAR CAME TO MALIBU."

Volume 6 | Number 6

THE DAY WAR ✳✳✳ CAME TO MALIBU

BY BILL CLEARY

In the gray of early morning, the cars arrived at Malibu. Then came whispered commands, and dark figures unloaded heavy equipment from the backs of trucks, from the tops of smaller vehicles. A dozen fires flickered down along the sand; above the raging surf came the tattoo of marching feet. War had been declared. But the weapon-shapes that loomed ominously in predawn darkness were but the finned missiles of wave riding; the soldiers were barefoot, and the war would be a friendly one—"Windansea," "Long Beach," "Haggerty's," "Hope Ranch," "Malibu" . . . hardly the names of regiments. But in the beginning, no one knew there would be real fighting.

DEWEY WEBER: "Dora and Fain were out for blood. They weren't fooling around; they realized that it was here they had made their reputation; hey, we're fighting for that number-one slot at Malibu Beach. Each wanted to be king; both wanted the Malibu throne. With Mickey and Johnny on that inside lineup, I didn't want anything to do with it—not because I thought I'd have been lowering myself to get in there and compete for applause, but because I just wanted to surf the best way I knew how. I take surfing as a sport. The AAU may not recognize it . . . but I do.

"I remember one wave I had picked up at the outside point and had ridden all the way inside where Mickey and Johnny took off. I was in back of them in the soup all the way to the beach, watching what was going on up in front. Mickey was working back and forth between the curl and the soup—he was shouting at Fain all the way, 'Get off my wave! What are you doing on my wave? Get off!' and Fain, of course, had a few things to say in return. And just as we hit the shorebreak, Dora shouted, 'Get off my wave or I'll cut your head off!' And he meant it. He dropped to the bottom and swung the board around, missing Fain by inches—so close his hair blew up as the board whizzed past!"

JOHNNY FAIN: "There was a big set, and one was close to 6 feet. That was the 'Truth Wave.' Mickey and I took off. I was in front. The wave was perfect, and I started climbing and dropping immediately. Mickey was behind, and I didn't know what he'd try to do, but he decided to maneuver like me. Of course, he couldn't, and when he followed me, he caught an edge and fell off, and I had the whole wave to myself all the way to the beach. The Truth Wave really set my maneuverability apart from Dora's. It was a battle—the Black Knight against the White Knight—and I won.

"But the Black Knight [Dora] thought he could get even on the next wave. I was in front . . . suckered him back into the whitewater and then I leaped to the nose. I was hung up there . . . it was perfect. I was on top of the world! But the Black Knight scrambled out of the curl, sputtering and stammering and cursing. And when I felt those icy fingers along the seat of my pants, I knew it was all over."

KATHY LIENHARD
SUNSET'S GLOW
PHOTO: RON STONER

JOYCE HOFFMAN
ON TIP, ON TOP
PHOTO: RON STONER

MIMI MUNROE, KATHY LACROIX
AND FELLOW COMPETITORS
1965 EAST COAST CHAMPIONSHIPS
PHOTO: RON STONER

Although women had played a vital role in surfing since Polynesian antiquity, features like this one helped foster stereotypes that would inhibit female surfers for years to come.

Volume 5 | Number 5

SURFER GIRLS

"Why does everyone make such a big thing of girl surfers?" "My friend and I were pounced upon by a dozen girls in a frenzy of vandalism." "In my opinion, the girls who run around looking like shaggy dogs dressed in gunny sacks aren't true to the sport." "I myself enjoy girl surfers." "Why not soften up, you guys?" Girls participating in the sport of surfing have aroused controversy to say the least. Many of the male surfers object strongly to "their" world being invaded by the girls. They feel that the closest girls should get to surfing is the beach. Most girls, of course, feel that this is unfair. Some even go so far as to think that the boys should help them carry their boards down to the surf and retrieve lost boards when they get wiped out!

Although the male surfers' opinions on girls also vary widely, the general feeling on the subject is this: Surfing is an individual sport, and the girls who want to surf should learn the traditions and courtesies along with the function of the sport. Just because she's a girl, she should not expect extra rights and privileges on the wave. There's nothing worse than an inexperienced girl ruining a good ride by dropping in on the shoulder right in front of a surfer coming off a hot section. On the other hand, the surfer who got dropped in on should calm his temper long enough to explain to the girl (in a nice manner) proper wave conduct. One young surfer summed up everything by saying, "Girls are OK as long as they don't get in the way and if they don't get any better!"

A response to racism, SURFER-style.

Volume 8 | Number 1

BLACK AND WHITE PHOTOGRAPHY

BY PATRICK McNULTY

Strangely, the picture that has produced the most reader response over the years had nothing to do with surfing. It was a shot that ran as part of the coverage of South African surfing. The caption simply stated, "Durban's beaches are segregated so this native youngster can't join these three surfers . . . for a little fun in the surf."

Response was tremendous. Letters poured into SURF POST. Many readers were critical of any policy of racial discrimination. Others—mostly from South Africa—defended the philosophy of keeping races separated. From Johannesburg, Keith Hosking demanded:

"Why don't you guys think before writing such trash?"

The South African position, essentially, is that Negroes are afforded separate but equal surfing facilities, and besides, blacks don't like surfing anyway. Some Americans agreed. From Jacksonville, Florida, Jackson Lanhart said:

"The beaches are practically segregated here in Jacksonville . . . the whites stay with the whites, and the blacks with the blacks . . . this way everybody's happy. . . ."

A dissenting opinion came from Cecil Robbins II, who does most of his surfing at South Hampton, Long Island. Robbins wrote:

"I am a Negro surfer . . . so what would happen if I and a group of my white friends go to Durban? I can't see any reason why I'd have to troop 200 yards down the beach just because I've got more pigment in my skin and a coarser grade of hair. That's not white supremacy—it's stupidity."

So what does all this have to do with surfing?

The photographer who took the picture—SURFER's roving Ron Perrott—gave this reason:

"The critics all lost sight of the key word in the caption: 'JOIN.' SURFER is an international magazine read by surfers of many races. If there is any restriction—whether political, religious or local—that hinders the free movement of any surfer, and if this regulation affects surfing or beaches, obviously it must be mentioned."

The concern of all of us—whether surfers or not—for human dignity and equality should not be confined to Durban or Watts or Grenada, Mississippi. We live in a world made incredibly small by the intercontinental ballistic missile. What happens in Cicero, Illinois, on the sweaty banks of the Congo River, or at Dairy Beach in Durban can affect all of us—whether we're paddling surfboards or not. Since more and more countries are acquiring the ultimate weapon and the means to deliver it, mankind soon may face the dilemma of living together peacefully—or not living at all.

Even so, SURFER's concern is with only one small aspect of living—surfing. And that brings us to the point of this editorial.

SURFER has always fought any force that would hamper any surfer from enjoying his sport anywhere in the world. Therefore, when a surfer is excluded from a surfing break for any reason—whether at Dairy Beach, Trestles, or Ocean City, New Jersey—SURFER will call attention to this injustice.

And, incidentally, a good tan has always been a status symbol in the sunny world of surfing. So a dark skin pigment is perhaps the weakest reason for limiting a surfer's activity in the water.

DURBAN, SOUTH AFRICA
PHOTO: RON PERROTT

THE HIGH PERFORMERS

By Bill Cleary

Photographed by Ron Stoner

DESIGN/LEO BESTGEN

FEATURING

☆ TOP TURNS ☆ BOTTOM TURNS ☆
TIP TURNS ☆ ROLLER-COASTERS ☆
& CIRCLE STALLS ☆ PLUS
FIN SPINS & RE-ENTRIES

This "mod" look at American surfing's performance leaders, by Bill Cleary, was written before the 1966 World Contest, where Australian Nat Young upset the whole applecart.

Volume 8 | Number 1

THE HIGH PERFORMERS

BY BILL CLEARY

Nuuhiwa
Hakman
Sutherland
Young
Carroll
Kanaiaupuni
And many, many more!!!

These are the new gods. The old ones were built by word of mouth; their exploits grew into heroic myths, and their names gave testimony to that colorful era when every surfer on the coast knew every other surfer on the coast by his first name. But the seasons pass, and the list of high performers under the age of 18 grows steadily longer; their standing in the eyes of the world is compiled quite accurately by tabulating machines following each officially sanctioned competition. They were born to it; the old gods were not.

And while the images of the pioneer performers such as Phil Edwards and Miklos F. (Chapin) Dora III grow dimmer and darker, Johnny Fain is still here crowing and bantering: "Mickey had me brainwashed. He told me I didn't need these contests. But he was wrong. Everything depends on contests now. Everything. Mickey's in the past now. He's an old man. I'd stay in the archives, too. With the cobwebs and things. . . ."

What about it, Mickey?

"I don't want to be a statistic," he replies. "I already feel like I'm inside the San Onofre Time Tunnel. . . ."

But what of tomorrow?

"I'm trying to find all sorts of new things to do on the wave," says David [Nuuhiwa]. "Spinning out on purpose when I was inside the tube was one thing . . . and I can do that almost any time I want now, when I'm going left. Another thing was my roller coaster. When a section came down, guys just tried to duck under it, so I did just the opposite. I'd go up the wave as hard as I could and then all down with it as it broke. Yeah . . . I guess I'm always looking for new things to do. All sorts of impossible things that just might come true."

Tell us, David. How does it feel to be told that the entire sport of surfing is following you?

"Ahhhh . . . are you kidding?"

"Hurry-Hurry-Hurry.
Step right up, folks,
See the greatest show of the century!
New stars with feats never before attempted
Right before your very eyes
In the Center Arena. . . ."

PETER JOHNSON
PHOTO: RON STONER

CORKY CARROLL
PHOTO: RON STONER

Written in response to Cleary's "High Performers" piece, this flag-waving diatribe by Sydney surf journalist John Witzig fanned flames of rivalry that still smolder today.

Volume 8 | Number 2

WE'RE TOPS NOW

BY JOHN WITZIG

"The High Performer?" Rubbish! That's all that can be said about that story in the last issue—Rubbish! Rubbish! Rubbish!

After our Nat Young completely dominated competition at the World Surfing Championships in San Diego, we might well have expected a more accurate assessment of California surfing than "The High Performers." Yet not, since this history is indicative to an absolute degree of the California scene as a whole. Has everyone forgotten that David was beaten? Thrashed?

Up pours the smoke. To laud, to defy, to obscure. To obscure the fact that everything the pedestal of California surfing is being built upon means—nothing!

"The whole sport is following Nuuhiwa now" . . . "and another thing was my roller coaster." *My* roller coaster, David? My? Ha! McTavish has been doing roller coasters for years.

Off with the rose-colored spectacles and look beyond the David. If everyone is not too conditioned by the propaganda: STOP. Reassess. Establish the real value in California surfing.

"Tell us, David . . . how does it feel to be told that the whole sport of surfing is following you?"

Are you kidding?

"Nat will thrash Nuuhiwa and make Bigler look like a pansy." These were the words of Bob Cooper when he saw Nat at Rincon in the week prior to the World Championships in San Diego. It was far more than a superficial comment when Cooper noted, "I haven't seen power surfing since I was in Australia." Cooper knew that Nat and Drouyn were not two isolated instances but were indicative of the new school of thought in Australia.

What is the future? We're on top and will continue to dominate world surfing. California surfing is so tied and stifled by restrictions that are its own creation, and the other countries simply do not have the necessary ability.

What chance is there that California will free itself of its encumbrances? This is something that I cannot answer. General social conditions will continue to exercise an influence over the surfing scene. The drug situation is something that cannot be ignored. While surfing progresses, the creative era is being credited to those who participate and, indirectly, because they participate, cannot forsee much change. Strangely enough, the effect of these stimulants seems to have a depressant effect on challenge and aggression. I felt like yelling, "Let yourself go; take a chance." But as is the pattern, this was not to be. Everyone was so confined, so under control, so absolutely without the apparent freedom to express.

An end must come to this monotony. Vigor will replace lassitude; aggression will replace meek submission. The dynamic will force an end to the commonplace. Power will be the word, and surfing will be surfing.

NAT YOUNG
CHANGING THE SPORT'S DIRECTION AT THE 1966 WORLD CONTEST IN SAN DIEGO
PHOTO: RON STONER

A world of waves: Ron Perrott, SURFER's first "foreign correspondent," on one of his classic early explorations.

Volume 8 | Number 5

SURFING THE SEYCHELLES

BY RON PERROTT

Before loading our gear into the trimaran, I posted a letter back to SURFER Magazine in California for that essential ingredient of any trip: money.

Surfing the Seychelles. I've got me a good live surfer and a sturdy 46-foot trimaran (the biggest in Africa). I'll send SURFER the bill at the end of the month!

We're sailing out of Durban Wednesday afternoon, which leaves just a day and a half to pack the old tropical kit, buy some mosquito repellent, swim for a few training laps in the baths—just in case the fiberglass gets ripped off the hulls in one of our 40-knot bursts of exuberance.

The trip to the Seychelles should take a month. Was talking to some splendid fellows down at the old yacht club the other night, and they said there's definitely surf in the Seychelles. Several islands in the group are volcanic in origin, with gently sloping rock sides approaching the sea. This time of year, there's also large ground swells around (gulp!), which all sounds just great for the cause (the cause being to make money, naturally!). So when you're in that oak-paneled retreat, think of me, mate—salt-caked lips cracking under the merciless sun, down to a cup of water a day, weevils in the hardtack, scurvy breaking out all over. The things I do for SURFER Magazine!

So, after all that nice, polite, informative chitchat comes, as you know, the oh-so-hard word: money. I'll be delighted if, on arriving at the Seychelles, there are vast stacks of SURFER bread waiting. So just seize your pen, crank out one of those pretty pieces of paper with the perforations and all that black ink that says "Pay to the order of Ron Perrott X American dollars," then sign it and, still with pen in hand, lower it slowly just above that line there . . . and write that gas name: HAPPINESS!

War was hell, even for surfers.

Volume 8 | Number 6

WE GET LETTERS

ART BY RICK GRIFFIN

Dear SURFER Magazine:

I'm sitting here in these funny green clothes that weren't designed for this weather. It's hot and humid, and I'm uncomfortable, and my Uncle Sam asks me to do some pretty unreasonable things. But my SURFER Magazine is smiling up at me. Let me try to explain to you what SURFER means to me over here.

After having lived inside this copy of SURFER for too many months, its torn cover reminds me of:

A friend waking me up, scratching the screen, "Hey, it's 7 o'clock, fool. Get up—the surf's up!"

Dew-covered grass in the front yard that makes my feet sting.

A ride that made me forget all the others.

Standing around a fire on the beach.

Getting sleepy at work because I surfed all morning.

Spending 75 gas-money cents on a copy of SURFER at the market—knowing that the 75 cents was one more trip to the surf, but also realizing that it was a SURFER-vicarious trip to Hawaii, Africa or someplace new.

SURFER speaks to me and I listen. It can take me on a time-space surf trip in minutes.

SURFER Magazine is all that behind torn-corner covers.

Thank you,

STEVE CARD
SAIGON, VIETNAM

Santa Barbara's eccentric surfing genius was so far ahead of his time that when this profile was printed, most surfers had no idea what he was talking about.

Volume 8 | Number 6
THE LEGEND OF GEORGE GREENOUGH

BY BILL CLEARY

"On a big wave, you can pull it down to a 60-degree angle, all the way over until you start dragging your shoulder. That's two Gs, but you'll hardly notice it if you're concentrating on the wave. I don't know how far I've gone beyond that, but it's gotten to the point where it has started to hurt and things have started to break. I had one board start to collapse on me one time. I let off the power when I felt it start to go, and I came out of the turn all right. . . ."

Then, without a pause, Greenough launched into a description of one well remembered ride close to the very limit. "It's a 10-foot wave—a thick, heavy, powerful wave. And you've driven 20 feet ahead of the curl . . . then you come around left again and put it right on the floor. You're going as fast as you can, head-on, straight into that tube! You're right at the top, and at the last possible second, you peel off and drop like an airplane, diving. You get railed-in tight; you get everything set up . . . get the suspension loaded; everything's twisted and bent to the maximum like a spring . . . and then you bring on the forces. Slowly. You come into the turn: brushing the white water—going to the bottom—banking harder and harder—still dropping. Then you hit the turn and start climbing, and you begin setting up your target. The target is high; you've got to tighten that turn. Now you're really flying because you began accelerating from the time you were 20 feet out in front of the curl, and you've come all the way back left, and you've driven all the way to the bottom. Your speed is tremendous! And now when you pull it down, you are very much aware of the forces. Your shoulder is only three or four inches from the face, and in your mind you say, 'Take it more. There's more power. You can't kill this wave!' And you pull it down even harder, and suddenly your foot feels like it's going to break, and your head is pushed so far down you're straining to see over the board at the target…and you know there is a lot of something pushing down on you."

GEORGE GREENOUGH
THREE Gs AT RINCON
PHOTO: BERNIE BAKER

FLEA SHAW
*RIGHT COAST STYLE AT THE EAST COAST
CHAMPIONSHIPS, COCOA BEACH, 1966*
PHOTO: RON STONER

MICKEY DORA
SURFING'S REBEL WITHOUT A PAUSE
PHOTO: SURFER ARCHIVES

Mickey Dora, surfing's dark prophet, the enigmatic, nonconformist, slightly nefarious counterpart to the sunny, Beach Boys image of California surfing, in one of his rare essays.

Volume 8 | Number 6

MICKEY ON MALIBU

BY MICKEY DORA

I'm grateful SURFER came to the source this time. Usually they obtain information about the Dora character from their paid stooges on the *Play Surf* editorial staff. Cheap gossip usually is the rule—especially with that star reporter Bill Cleary—one of the great frauds of our times. This guy deserves the SURFER Pulitzer Prize for double-talk, hot-air articles he contrives about me. Sometimes I wonder how many minds believe the lies he writes about me—for example, the so-called reporting job he did on the Malibu contest a year ago.

You know, Cleary old boy, someday you're going to find out I'm not public property and my private life is my own business. I'm not a commodity of yours to use in your cheap quick-buck articles. Last year's contest is a perfect example of using my name to save a no-wave, miserable day's judging on your part. Remember, Cleary, I'm not obligated to you or anybody else. I ride waves for my own kicks, not yours.

I know SURFER must be jammed up for a deadline. The annual Huntington Beach best seller was a smashing flop. What is the magazine going to do without all those straight-off photos in the white water? All those thousands of inland-slave-mentality imbeciles who go goose-stepping into that helmeted restrictive lifeguard state takeover that they call a contest.

All right, why not express myself? The price is just about right for what it's worth.

Malibu, personally, is my perfect wave. Naturally, when it's breaking correctly. And when it's right, it's right in the palm of my hand. These waves will never change, only the people on them. And that's what I remember, the waves I ride, not the crud that floats around them. Somebody out there must understand what I'm saying, and others won't. Like any good thing, the idealism can't last forever, and that's what's happening to Malibu (understatement of the decade).

When I talk to guys who I think are in the know, who are still riding waves for the sheer freedom they offer all of us, these same guys look at me as if I were out of my mind to run the gauntlet every time I want to express myself in the water. Their concept of Malibu today is a complete Valley takeover, a fantasy of insanity filled with kooks of all colors, super egomania running rampant, fags, finks, pork chop–ism and a thousand other social deviations. The tragic thing is they're all true; these guys are right, up to a point.

It's very hard to stand up to all the put-downs and heat I go through to work a few waves over. But, I do have my moments, and that neutralizes this whole illusion. However, I can't help feeling there's something happening and things are not going to stay the same. New philosophies are taking hold. There is a great deal of change occurring in certain segments of the sport, and I hope you want the same things I want: freedom to live and ride nature's waves, without the oppressive hang-up of the mad insane complex that runs the world and this sick, sick war.

Things are going to change drastically in the next year or so for all of us whether we like it or not. Maybe a few will go forward and make it a better world.

These are incredible times.

Thank God for a few free waves.

By 1967, change was in the wind, even at surfing's traditional winter gathering in Hawaii.

Volume 9 | *Number 2*

HAWAII'S NORTH SHORE

BY CRAIG LOCKWOOD / ART BY RICK GRIFFIN

THE NORTH SHORE HILTON

"But I like to sleep on the floor," says McNulty, on the Japanese mat. "I heard once that sleeping on the floor was good for your back."

"No," says Fain, "that's sleeping without a pillow. . . . That's food for your neck."

"How come you've got all the pillows, then, Fain?" Neumann wants to know. Fain points to his neck and tells him that it helps his whiplash.

"What whiplash?" ask Neumann.

"Pipeline whiplash," says Fain.

Bodies are stretched out, but nobody's sleeping. Surf excitement hasn't ended. The new thing is talked over, talked around, discussed and evaluated. The consensus: there's less hostility and more cooperation. . . genuine interest and commitment to what's being accomplished.

The surfer with the beard leans forward, pushing a board out of the way so he can speak. . . .

"Last year it was really getting tight, aggressiveness and hostility and fear. All that stuff. But now we've broken the sound barrier."

"The sound barrier?"

"The sound barrier is all the vocal intellectualizing that was going on. We've stopped listening to that. We've broken through ego and begun to communicate with each other. We're beginning to get where it is.

"It is old feuds ending and people realizing that they don't have to be bitter. That's part of the new thing, like what happened to Fain at Pipeline."

"What was that, Johnny?" I asked.

Fain grins and tells it like it was: The Pipeline was working and the cameras were cranking. Fain and his board had parted company down the face of a Banzai widowmaker. Fain had disappeared into the white water, but the board, tracking, had continued on. The heavy lip of the wave then caught the board and broke it; nicely, cleanly, halved. Fain, shaken, but in one piece, swam in. Fain's face clouds over and he said:

"I mean—you know—what else could happen? What further calamities? I'd just lost a $170 speed board in a fraction of a second, nearly got ground, drowned and cut to bits, crawled up to shore and . . ."

And then . . . like the Fates descending from the roof in a Greek tragedy, comes:

". . . a big, hairy, mean-looking ape!"

"Who was it? The abominable surfman?" I asked.

"No!" says Fain, hoarse-loud . . . then dropping off to a stage whisper. . . . "It was D-O-R-A."

Everyone hung on John's next sentence.

"He was walking his strange walk down the beach, zeroing in on me, right? What else could happen now? Dora was the last straw. I was ready to check out right there."

And what does Dora do? Does he come up and point and laugh? Does he throw sand at Fain and run? No, he walks up, consoles Fain and commiserates about the board. Nobody can believe it.

"That's the new thing," says the bearded surfer.

STEVE BIGLER
AND A BIG GUN AT SUNSET
PHOTO: JOHN SEVERSON

LEFT TO RIGHT: BOB CLOUTIER,
JOEY CABELL AND GEORGE DOWNING
MINI-GUNNING, HALEIWA
PHOTO: PETER FRENCH

BOB McTAVISH
HAWAII, 1967
PHOTO: RON STONER

Australian Bob McTavish was the primary architect of the "shortboard revolution," and his psychedelic call to arms caught the American surf industry by surprise.

Volume 9 | *Number 3*

THE CHALLENGE FROM DOWN UNDER

BY JOHN WITZIG

McTAVISH:

LADIES AND GENTLEMEN AND CHILDREN-OF-THE-SUN: Today, surfing's main school is to turn the board, walk to move out, get forward for trim, adjust a little across the board, backpedal like a logroller to haul the board into a cutback type. Noseride, slide white water, stick your body into any nearby mass of fluff. **CALL IT INVOLVED**, "in," New Era, high performance, aggressive. Call it anything. Plenty of thrills in it, deep moving out, but—oh!—in a straight line again. Nice wall. Walk up some, hold back on the inside rail, let it go! Walk up for full trim. Moving like crazy! But . . . in a straight line. **BREAK OUT FROM THE STRAIGHT LINE.** Go

fly . . . go free . . . up, up and away down the barrel . . . down down and up! Drop, bounce thrust . . . up, down thrust . . . cut!

SOUNDS BRONZER. HOW PLEASE?

Get yours from on the all-new **FANTASTIC '68 MODEL VERTICAL PERFORMANCE CUT-DOWN THRUST-UP INNER SPACE PROBING ZAPPER.**

Kid's crazy.

SHALL I EXPLAIN FURTHER OR JUST LET THE NEWS SLOWLY, INEVITABLY CREEP OVER THIS CARVE-UP, KIDDY? I SHALL PUT IT DOWN; HE MAY PICK UP AS HE SO DESIRES.

Here's putting down news. Surfing equipment evolution has

swung into a new phase. A huge new breakaway direction has sprung out of the conventional surfboard move. The entire thought behind this new flow is freedom. This is not surfboard riding. This is wave riding. These are not surfboards; these are new vessels. A board is a rigid flat plank for standing poised upon, balancing, defying waves from flinging. The little wide-back machines, vessels or flying saucers are mind vehicles, just like our bodies. Performing, like part of your body, the new unit will take your consciousness many fantastic places, in some fantastic ways.

How? Elimination of two feet of board. Limitation of walking. Sounds like you're just going to hang around the tail. Right. Hang around upside-down, sideways, doing 360 degrees, flying. You see, the turn area doubles as a planing area. It's wide and flat. Many square inches of plane—acceleration and speed. Fraction of a second from banking to full planing. Maximum speed one-half second from banked edge.

You can get yourself from some deep hole, out and up under the lip, in the blink of an eyelid. Up under the lip, the speed you have allows you to bank up under there, much like a toboggan in an ice trough deal. Centrifugal force. The force that gave you the speed in the first place. That wide, wide tail will not mush in. That short length (7 feet and up) can be spun into a cutback without ever digging and sinking. Ridiculous maneuverability. Especially the offsets.

Vertical performance. Broken the straight line at last. Replace noseriding as World's No. 1 fad? Why not? It's limitless.

Mind, Body, Soul; Surfer, Board, Wave; Total and Complete Involvement. Let the mind unshackle; set it free. Let it stroll, run, leap, laugh in gardens of crystal motion and sun and reality. Talk with the caretaker on the Plastic Telephone. Weave and pain with the hand of your imagination, with the fingers of your body, brush of fiberglass. See that cavity up there? I'd love to be there, upside-down, carvin' off a cutback. Hey! The horizon's going over, up! Wow!! Sssswishssss, sswoooop!!

Toes pressed through wax job. Stomach in upper reaches of chest cavity. Feeling the bounce of the reentry.

Ridden the explosion of the close-out today? Yes, the 360 after the weightless was rather good. Dragged my whole bum in one of those backhands. Free? Yes, thanks. Share this one. Try dual tube? You call the turns. The circus is in town. Yes, I'd love a rose?"

THE POINT AT JEFFREYS BAY
SURFING'S FIRST LOOK
PHOTO: RON PERROTT

New wave "discoveries" rewrote surfing's maps on a bimonthly basis.

Volume 9 | *Number 4*

JEFFREYS BAY

Now the jackpot question: name a fabulous right point break off the tip of a continent noted for zebras, wild Zulus and people with transplanted hearts. . . .

Let's see; that must be Africa, and. . . .

Time is running out. . . .

It's coming to me . . . I saw it in that movie—something about a Cape. . . .

Just a few seconds left. . . .

Let's see, a fantastic right point break off a point of Africa with a name that starts with "Cape. . . ."

Almost time. . . .

I've got it—Cape St. Francis . . . the perfect wave of Bruce Brown's *Endless Summer.* Who could forget Mike Hynson and Robert August getting those endless, locked-in rides?

Cape St. Francis? Is that your answer? You're wrong. The correct answer is Jeffreys Bay.

The world of the surfer was expanding, and in ways and places never imagined. Great Britain's national champ launched this memorable "surfari" down England's Severn River.

Volume 9 | *Number 4*

THE WORLD'S MOST UNUSUAL WAVE

BY RODNEY SUMPTER

The dart game stopped abruptly; a fellow with foam on his mustache stood frozen in the middle of the room holding a half-drained pint of English beer. The pubkeeper had both hands on the bar and, mouth open, was staring at me. The fellow throwing the darts paused, holding a feathered barb next to his right ear.

There I stood with my surfboard under my arm in the middle of a typical English pub on the banks of the Severn River. "What are these people staring at?" I thought to myself. "Haven't they ever seen a surfer before?"

The pubkeeper was the first to react. "What's that under your arm?" he asked. All eyes zeroed in on my 9-foot surfboard.

RODNEY SUMPTER
SLIDING THE SEVERN BORE
PHOTO: SIMONE SUMPTER

"Why, it's a surfboard, of course."

The pubkeeper blinked a couple times and then turned to the dart player and the beer drinker and said in a voice that meant, "Well, that explains everything": "A surfboard. He's carrying a surfboard."

The dart player mumbled something and threw a dart that hit the edge of the board. The man carrying the beer went over, sat at the bar and just shook his head. Finally, the pubkeeper looked at me and said in a very quiet voice, "Why are you carrying a surfboard around in the middle of England?"

"I'm going surfing tomorrow," I said. "I'm going to ride the Severn Bore. . . ."

. . . I came sweeping around a turn, just away from the bank at a town called Stone Beach—where the bore is biggest and strongest. Many people in the cottages close to the bank are forced to abandon their homes because of the gradual erosion of the river. The wave, moving over deep water, flattened off to a glassy 18 inches with a very short shoulder. I edged toward the nose to stay in the wave and moved close to the bank as trees, bushes and stumps came at me at an alarming speed. I ducked under a tree and then proned out and smashed through an overhanging bush. I stood up again, and the inside section of the bore smashed against the bank, hurling a mass of mud and foam sideways, flipping me over—wipeout!

Imagine, a wipeout in the middle of England. It was really wild. I remember hanging onto the board upside down and skidding across mud and then letting go of the board. I thought I'd stopped. I could hear the water boiling and booming, and when I opened my eyes for a split second, I discovered I was being pushed by the wave along the bank on my back toward a tree. I felt that I was going 20 miles an hour and, panic stricken, I grabbed at every branch and bush in a desperate effort to stop before slamming into the tree.

I slid and stopped beside the tree, and the bore smothered me with mud, grime and foam. For a moment, I had the panicky feeling that I'd never come up, as this is not just a single wave; it's the whole force of the Atlantic Ocean coming in at 12 miles an hour. In spite of the currents and turbulence, I popped out the back of the bore in much the same way as I would have a normal wave. I was covered with mud and grime and bushes as I crawled to the safety of the bank. I found my board tangled up in branches and, putting it under my arm, I walked away dirty, bruised and bedraggled, from one of the wildest rides of my surfing career.

Where were Simone and the camera crew? Probably cruising a country road downstream waiting for me to appear around a bend. I trudged over a field looking for someone who might give me some directions back to the main road. I was really a mess, covered with mud and branches. My green wetsuit was ripped and torn. Only my board had come through unscratched.

Finally, I came across a small picturesque cottage nestled in the corner of a rolling English farm field. I knocked, and a little old lady answered the door. She looked at me standing there in my green wetsuit, my hair matted and full of Severn mud and branches. Wiping the grime from my face, I tried to flash my friendliest surfer smile.

But do you know what? A curious thing happened. Her eyes got very large, and she started to scream: little sounds, mouse-like squeaks that began high-pitched and got higher and higher and higher.

Then, still screaming, she turned and ran back into another room of the cottage and left me standing there wet and cold and wondering why the English sometimes act so strange when they run into a perfectly normal everyday surfer.

By 1968, SURFER artist Rick Griffin was a major force in California's psychedelic art scene—and hapless Murphy had his mind blown.

RICK GRIFFIN

FROM "ALMOND EYES," BY DREW KAMPION, VOL. 11, NO. 4

The other wave was Rick Griffin's. Not that it was really his wave, but he rode it, and in it there was one perfect moment: the wave hollowed out and fringing, raked a bit by the offshore for 20 feet ahead of him. Rick on his cruiser (or Charger), left hand directing ahead, long hair flying like a head full of snakes, just touching the lip of the wave, and another long snake of kelp waiting in the wall ahead of him, implanted like a fossil in the wall of a transparent cave, venomless and silent. Without time.

RICK GRIFFIN
MURPHY CREATOR AND SURFER'S DOMINANT ARTISTIC FORCE THROUGHOUT THE '60s

SURFER photographer Ron Stoner's travails boating into the perfect—and perfectly forbidden—surf beckoning from the private Hollister Ranch, south of California's Point Conception.

Volume 9 | *Number 5*

THE ADVENTURES OF A RANCH ADDICT

BY RON STONER

We pulled the boat up to Gaviota Pier and launched it. The boat was pretty old, a really narrow 15-footer with a low back—and with five of us and five surfboards and all of our supplies, it was only floating about 2 inches above the water. But we were stoked, so we started motoring up the coast, and it took us about two hours to make it to Cojo. The weather was great, and the place looked fantastic from the water, even though there wasn't any surf. By the time we got to

Cojo, it was getting windy: blowing offshore and cold. We beached the boat and sat around eating a lot of food until about 2 in the afternoon. By this time, the wind had blown up a few 1-footers, and Mark Hammond and I went out and tried to surf them. But the offshores were so strong you couldn't stay in the waves. The wind really started picking up, so we figured we should head back.

On the way up, it was smooth, and we found

trails through the kelp; but now the wind was so strong, the whole ocean started white-capping except where the thick kelp beds kept it smooth. It was either the whitecaps or the kelp beds, so Bill just cranked up his old rusty 20 horsepower job and tried to carve a trail right through the middle of all that kelp. After a few minutes, we looked back and the motor was on fire. And then it just conked out. We scooped up a lot of salt water and put the fire out.

MIKE HYNSON
CLASSICAL GLASS AT THE RANCH
PHOTO: RON STONER

But when we took the cowling off, the motor was all black and frozen from the heat, and things looked pretty hopeless. The wind was blowing even harder, and we were drifting outside, so we reached overboard and grabbed armfuls of kelp and tied our boat up. Our first mistake was tying it up stern first. And with this real low back to it, the water started splashing in faster than we could bail it out. The wind kept getting stronger and stronger, and the boat was filling up with water. About every half hour or so, we'd break loose from the kelp and we'd have to tie up again. Finally, we were about a mile outside, right on the edge of the kelp, and from then on it was just open sea and the sun was starting to go down. Once, when a train was going by, Mark Hammond tied a red towel to an oar and waved it, but it was getting too late in the afternoon for anyone to see us. I hated to look down because all the camera equipment was in the bottom of the boat covered with water. But by

this time, I was starting to worry about more than just the camera equipment.

We were bailing water with Dixie cups and losing ground fast. Kruthers had a paper bag over his head; the water was up to our waist, and the wind was getting stronger, so we put wetsuits on over our clothes. We figured the wind was probably 50 to 75 miles per hour, and all of a sudden, it seemed to get a little stronger and the boat kind of jerked and the wave broke over the back, and the boat went out from underneath us. As it sunk, we grabbed our boards and started paddling into the wind. When I stopped to look over my shoulder and thought of hundreds of dollars' worth of camera equipment going to the bottom, I lost about 10 yards headway, and I figured it was all over and we were doomed. But I just kept on paddling and paddling, and about a half hour later, I could feel sand in the wind and I knew we were getting close.

Finally, we made it to shore, and about a half hour later, as we huddled freezing in a gully, a helicopter landed to rescue us. The pilot said the winds were hurricane force, about 80 miles an hour, and the train that went by earlier in the afternoon reported us in trouble. The chopper flew Kruthers, Andrews and me down to Gaviota, and a rescue boat found our swamped boat and towed it back to the Gaviota Pier. From there I drove up and asked the ranch guard if he would let us drive in and get our friends who were stranded on the beach between Cojo and San Augustine. He said OK, and I parked at San Augustine and then ran up the beach to find Fury and Hammond. It was like trying to run with steel shoes into the wind. We finally found them, drove back and got the boat out of the water. By the time we hit Santa Barbara, we were completely exhausted. Jeff had a friend there, so we just crashed on his floor. The next day we drove home.

WAYNE LYNCH
THROUGH THE LOOKING GLASS
PHOTO: PAUL WITZIG

1968 surf savant Wayne Lynch from Australia expresses himself in this remarkable essay, written when he was only 16.

Volume 9 | Number 6

DIGGING IT

BY WAYNE LYNCH

This is an article about my opinions of my own surfing and society. Nothing more, nothing less. Surfing today has become far too political and restrictive. Organizations have seemed, in many cases, to have drifted away from their natural purpose. This will change when the sprocket of generations tricks over one more cog.

McTavish says California has had it. Personally, I think Australia has had it. Not as a place, but as a community. Surfing has turned to politics. Every surfing magazine contains politics. Creative surfing in many cases has been forgotten. Why, I don't know. Maybe it will all flow over! I hope so. The Australian surfing scene has changed. It's lost its drive and creativity. There is too much hate and jealousy. Top

surfers have spread apart, leaving a gaping hole in the progress of the nation. It went so well for a while. Everyone was digging surfing for what it is. Everyone together, everyone understood, and now everyone's gone. They are still around, mind you, but they are all separate, some digging, some not.

SURFER is too sensationalized but always contains three or four excellent articles on guys and places over there. Talking to guys who have been over there, they say the people are wonderful. I believe it; I know some. Surfing is very underdeveloped. There is so much more to be done. Infinitely more. Vertical climbing to be more of what it is. Drifting deep, foils for fins to give power from deep inside. Foiled boards! How about 360-degree turns? How about riding the face of a perfect wave right up an' over? A complete loop. Centrifugal force. That bitchin' little helper of us all. Wow, it's so inspiring to think of it all! To abandon the straight line. To slice that line up. Imagine trying to judge some kid in a contest who drops down a good 8-foot wave, powers through the bottom, pop goes his fin as he controls the whole thing and his foiled rail. Zap! Wow! The acceleration: amazing! He ascends the face on an 80-degree angle to horizontal, pushes the board onto the other Vee at the top, and swirls the whole thing just as vertically down. Once at the bottom, with toe pressure and

who knows how many Gs, he powers again into the complete cylindrical cavity. This time he doesn't bank off but holds it, everything or maybe nothing, because so much power, and, kathunk! The board so quickly, yet so surely, has ridden that unused face of the wave. Over, way over. Speed and force! A free fall. Slap. Bottom, I guess. Then pop out the bottom gasping for air. Lungs and ribs aching. But he doesn't stop. Again he drop the fin, shoots himself into the loop. Ahh! A cover-up. Now he sights the next movements of the wave. So carefully. From the top, he runs the board into some sort of fantastic speed in deep. Force has put him low into the board. He banks. With hand on rail, he guides the board and again the fin causes a swivel. At the top, the speed is unbelievable, toes hard on the inside. Hard, harder, hardness on softness. Hope it's not too soft. Then, with a last wrench of the rail, he drives down the wave on the inside of his upward track. A 360-degree turn. From here, he puts many arcs on the face of the wave, 180-degree cutbacks, and finishes it off with a reentry. How do you judge that? Why even try to? These things can be done. I have tried and succeeded a handful of times in doing them. But separately. In years to come, these things will be done over and over. How do you judge or label it? I won't worry about that, 'cause I'll be out there digging it.

WAYNE AT 16
PHOTO: DAVE SINGLETARY

Volume 9 | *Number 6*

REFLECTION

The promised sand
Forbidden land
Restraining line
With sharpened spine
NO SURFING HERE:
The warning sign
Perfection waves
Reflecting mind:
Humanity
Could be so blind

— ERWIN DENCE

"BOMMY" BEACHUM
LONGBOARD STYLE
PHOTO: RON STONER

JO JO PERRIN
EXTREME V-LAND VECTOR
PHOTOS: ART BREWER

The late 1960s was a period of self-examination—and the reexamination of old values. Drew Kampion and Tom Morey were two of the era's most eloquent voices.

Volume 10 | *Number 2*

VECTORS AND VARIATIONS

and now it's 1969 or '70...
hard to tell because everything is flowering together now:
riders and waves
colors
cutbacks and turns
noserides and stalls
climbs and drops,
all connected by the tendon of fluidity;
big waves, small waves
glassy and windblown waves,
all gush open under the arcing of the plastic machines.
plastic weapons and brown soldiers
meeting the green, blue, orange, white challenge.
what is art?
define your cause!
where is the word for surfing?
is it cooper: infinite vectors in conflict,
yet at equilibrium?
is it dora: contraction at the epicenter, fusion vs. fission?
is it frye: silk repetition, flagrant indulgence in a
perfect groove?
is it bigler: photographic duplication of da vinci's
weapons; contemporary primate?
is it nuuhiwa: flaunting in the silence of microcosm?
is it carroll: redefining vs. refining, a question of
motivation and beautiful pragmatism?
is it mctavish: spawn of witzig; carving interrogatives
on blue celluloid?
is it young: incredible inertia, seldom latent, always
with direction?
is it cabell: embryonic involvement, oedipal conflict?
is it all of these?
assimilate, devour, osmos, indulge, undefine or
redefine or just define or divine?
or man in his finest hour?   — *DREW KAMPION*

To me/for me, surfing is a way of exercising as hard as a basketball player but never smelling like a basketball player.

It is a way of cooling off in the summer,
a way of getting warm in the winter,
a way of competing (and thereby learning about such competition) in a punitive society, one without written rules or police,
a way of overcoming fear (and the fearlessness/guts/or however you call it extends into one's entire being),
a way of achieving real genuine fun thrills,
a way of clowning, fighting, wooing, outfoxing,
a way of experiencing hunting and experiencing being hunted,
It is a liquid/solid tinkertoy set/sculpture set/skating rink,
It is a more enjoyable bath than baths or showers,
It is a human factors research lab,
It is a sales office,
It is an arena,
It is a washing machine,
It is a toilet,
It is the field in which I work,
It is the world of most of my friends,
It is the focal activity of my life,
What is writing about surfing? Like, writing about surfing is drawing the sun with one color.   — *TOM MOREY*

SUNRIDE DRIFT
PHOTO: BRAD BARRETT

Mickey Dora's deliberately incendiary "last interview" accurately predicted the rise and fall of several major epochs, adding considerably to the Dora mystique.

Volume 10 | *Number 4*

DORA INTERVIEW

BY SAM REID

WHAT PART DOES SURFING PLAY IN YOUR LIFE TODAY?
When there's surf, I'm totally committed; when there's none, it doesn't exist.

WHAT CHANGES HAVE YOU WITNESSED DURING THE COURSE OF YOUR SURFING CAREER?
First of all, I have no "career." I was here before, and I'll be here after. As to the occurrences of change, I've observed a multitude. Briefly, I've seen the dead origins, genesis, the hours of recession, and we are all soon to undergo the sport's demise in the immediate future.

COULD YOU CLARIFY THESE VARIOUS PERIODS?
The dead origins consisted of the 250-plus redwoods and their wined-out "T" square build grapplers, who fantasized themselves to be the magnates of an illusionary Polynesian culture. Bicep flexes, ukulele playing, tight trunks and body grease typified the period. I've only mentioned this era since it is frequently portrayed and glamorized as the birth of the sport, etc. Those guys weren't concerned with the effective riding of waves, and people today should realize this. The genesis days were a time of innovation, creation, birth and individuality. The recession embodies the passage of time from the genesis period's end to the present. Essentially, mediocrity and rehashed mediocrity. To the unenlightened eye, things have constantly been progressing; however, close scrutiny reveals the modern world to be a mere illusion of opulence, grandeur and good feelings. People currently are riding the calm before the storm, and have been lulled into such a false sense of security that they view current occurrences as if they possess some sort of solidified foundation. They are viewing illusions as truth. The death is the fall of the above mentioned illusionary society, values and prosperity. It will also entail a general shattering of the weak.

PRECISELY WHEN WAS THIS "GENESIS" PERIOD, AND WHAT MADE IT SO IMPORTANT TO THE SPORT'S DEVELOPMENT?
It took place approximately from 1949 to 1954. This was the period of the only true innovation of design concepts and riding techniques the sport has ever endured. At this point, a few beings rebelled against the World War II shell-shocked casualties, redwoods, and embarked upon the direction surfing is still on. This departure from the redwoods was led primarily by Bob Simmons.

Simmons' short, lightweight, controlled flow concepts and water release contours set up this period. Simmons' principles threatened the security of the redwood boys and caused him much ridicule. This scorn only drove Simmons and his adherents to greater heights and stages of development. Apparently, Simmons went too far in shaking up the status quo, since in 1954, Simmons drowned under mysterious and unlikely circumstances, ending the genesis movement. Of this period, Matt Kivlin's techniques, riding-wise, were the definite high point. Kivlin's mellow style and intricate knowledge of wave positioning set him apart from the multitude, past and present. Many have been heavily influenced by the Kivlin technique, myself included; however, none will ever be able to come close to this genius of style. Kivlin retired from surfing immediately after the killing of Simmons, and surfing began a period of intense mediocrity, which has strung out to the near past. Recently, however, a renaissance trend has occurred, resulting from the present reaction against the stagnation of inhibiting designs and wave-riding methods. Unfortunately, this period is going to be cut short by the previously mentioned collapse of surfing. Fortunately, out of the ashes of death, the surviving individualists will start a future "genesis" period which, hopefully, will get off on a better foot, due to their insight into the causes which felled society and the sport. However, restrictive conservatism may kill off these few survivors just as it once liquidated Simmons.

EXACTLY WHAT DO YOU MEAN BY THIS DEMISE OF SURFING?
Since Nov. 22, 1963, a curse has fallen upon this country. It has affected it internationally, as well as on the "home front." Since this tragic date, the mainland breaks have gradually worsened, and the ground swell has been relegated to the ranks of the unlikely. Cities burn, schools are sieged and overseas commitments increase. It's only a matter of time before this upheaval shall reach endeavors such as surfing. Monetarily, the manufacturers, publishers, clothes companies and cinematographers will all collapse due to overextension, insufficient funds and knowledge, just retribution and nature's cleansing. In short, the creeps who have worked the people over for years are going to fold. The only people to survive this fall will be the true independents, those who will have nothing to do with the upper echelon of this current illusionary prosperity. Any person who complies with the current ruling faction will only provoke his own downfall through corruption and association. People who play ball by reading publications such as this are dooming themselves to extinction.

WHY DO YOU FEEL THIS FALL IS GOING TO OCCUR?
The advent of "professionalism" to the sport will be the final blow. Professionalism will be completely destructive of any control an individual has over the sport at present. These few Wall Street flesh merchants desire to unify surfing only to extract the wealth. Under this "professional" regime, the wave rider will be forced into being totally subservient to the few in control in order to survive. The organizers will call the shots, collect the profits, while the wave rider does all the labor and receives little. Also, since surfing's alliance with the decadent big business interests is designed only as a temporary damper to complete fiscal collapse, the completion of such a partnership will serve only to accelerate the art's demise. A surfer should think carefully before selling his being to these "people," since he's signing his own death warrant as a personal entity.

MICKEY DORA
FRONTIER JUSTICE, MALIBU, 1968
PHOTOS: BRAD BARRETT

Filmmaker Greg MacGillivray and crew put European surfing firmly on the map with this timely travelogue.

Volume 10 | Number 4

EUROPE: GENESIS

BY MACGILLIVRAY/FREEMAN, MARK MARTINSON AND BILLY HAMILTON

Near the beach is a huge campground cubed up with bright blue tents—French Army surplus camouflage variety. A group of swimmers play in the shorebreak at the tail end of a perfect sandbar break. For years, they've played here while millions of perfect little coils unwound without a scar. Mark, Bill and Keith quickly paddle out and begin mauling the "hairy little cylinders." Jim and I set up still and movie cameras on shore. The waves are extraordinary—repetitious perfection, breaking in the same spot with the same shape every time. Mark is trying new things, but the square-tailed Vee is giving him some problems. He borrows Keith's roundtail for a few rides and doesn't want to give it back. But the situation changes rapidly, and in an hour, the waves are eaten by the tide. High tide, often 13 feet, can cause sandbar breaks to vanish or go someplace else. The cameras and boards are gathered up, and we search out Joel to tell him of our discovery. We find him at JoJo's, a sidewalk café at Chambre d'Amour. We take a seat at the sidewalk table with Joel, his wife Stella, Jacques Valls, Phillippe Gerard, and Marianne Nicolas. The café owner, JoJo, promptly steps up to the table with a stack of porcelain dishes and proceeds to toss them out like he was dealing cards, all the time belching out a great front of laughter. A few are dropped and break, but JoJo continues dealing until everyone has one. He then heaps a gigantic mound of spaghetti on each plate, and, still laughing, tells us that surfers are his worst customers…they don't catch very well. We tell Joel and friends about our new discovery, Castles, and then they tell us about a similar spot to the north called Hossegor. "Not many surfers go there. It's about an hour's drive," Joel adds, as we begin back to Isabel to prepare for the trip.

Tonight Mark writes home to Rich Harbour, giving him the first specifications of a new roundtail board tuned to Mark's surfing demands. Mark mails the letter immediately, and, just as quick, is anxious for a reply. "Chances are," says Bill, "you won't hear from Harbour tonight."

KEITH PAULL
CÔTE DU BASQUE
PHOTO: MacGILLIVRAY/FREEMAN

MARINES VERSUS SURFERS AT TRESTLES
PHOTO: RON STONER

Even as Vietnam raged, a war was being fought on the home front, with surfers and U.S. Marines clashing at Trestles, on San Clemente's Camp Pendleton.

Volume 10 | Number 5

TRESTLES

BY DREW KAMPION

The issue at stake is an absurd one: surfers do not wish to give up the privilege of floating in the Pacific Ocean adjacent to Camp Pendleton. The Marine Corps, because someone once said, "It is your ocean," has to maintain that ocean. This maintenance consists of ejecting surfers. You may get a fishing permit and kill fish at Trestles. You can get a camping permit along with it if you have pull, and litter the beach. Or you can be a Marine and train to recognize and annihilate your enemy there. But you can't be a surfer and float on it.

You can be a boat owner and boat through it, dragging a line, killing fish, spreading an aluminum minefield of beer cans. You can be an oil-tanker driver and dump gobs of tar all over it. You can be an oil company and spill your waste into it. You can be a sewage plant and pump your feces into it. But you can't be a surfer and float on it.

Obviously, there appears to be something happening here. It seems that surfing, a totally nondepletive, nondestructive sport, has been more or less singled out by the Jars. Perhaps it's because the thought of free bodies in a free ocean participating in a nondestructive, free activity is an excessive tax on the Marine mentality. Who knows?

It is possible that the Marines find the surfing philosophy temporarily abhorrent. It is all they have been trained to distrust. You don't salivate at the thought of freedom and brotherhood, or you get your hand slapped. Salivating is a pre-kill phenomenon.

This all adds up to something greater than what has gone into it: it is important that the surfers uphold their right to surf in these, and all, waters. It is important that surfers maintain themselves aloof from the storm-troop tactics of our brothers in khaki. It is important that everybody gets behind this Trestles thing and makes his voice heard to someone. Someone besides a fellow surfer.

While surfers surfed, a tumultuous world sometimes seemed to spin around them.

Volume 10 | *Number 5*

THE DAY THEY WALKED ON THE MOON

BY DREW KAMPION

The day they walked on the moon there was a contest at Oceanside. A 3A. Scheduled for the jetty but ending up south of the pier and starting out of gray, choppy, early light. A cold group on the beach and a few jerseyed surfers in the water. No breakfast yet, but stomach working up for it. Another 3A....

And all this time, 240,000 miles away, three men floated in a vacuum getting set for the big step. The module planted four-footed on the gray ash of the moon, the ladder dropping out and down, the hatch opening and the step stepping down its metallic web, then—KAZONK!—Jock hits the lip, fin slips out, spray and trash fly, the wall elasticizes, he pushes, fin grabs, section explodes, he carries over the top and falls armpit-deep in foam. And makes it! KABLOOEY! Preiss wiggle-waggles along a wall, faces a right coming head-on to his left. Cut out? Fly over? Hell, no: under it, then up through the crashing lid and over the falls for 43 points at least, because you don't go around making these things. Little knee-riding experience showing. SCREECH! Steve Schlickenmeyer comes around at the bottom of a 6-footer, his rail making the only water contact there is, like a thing in a groove, so you expect him just to sit there 360ing six or seven times, but he breaks it, bangs off the soft underside of a ceiling and comes around again off the bottom. Why does

he bother with a fin? He barely keeps it in the water long enough to twang it. Astronaut whatever-his-name was/is takes Step One, while these little plastic slithering sticks do a basting job on Earth's spiraling head spinners. The ballet is similar. The vehicles are at opposition. Surfboards are cleaner than rocket ships.

On this particular Sunday, Jock wins; Steve Schlickenmeyer is second and Scott Preiss is third. The day is colder and windier and wetter than it was earlier, and the beach dissolves back into sand as soon as the trophies are passed out. Enthusiasm is strained or absent. The trophies seem artificial appendages to the art of surfing. Pointless, anachronistic, obtrusive. This bit of art is worth so much metal and wood. Your bit is worth this much, etc. It all seems a bit blatant.

Home is a familiar dash. Campers crowding the highways. Family units in transit back to their homes to twist guts and raise calluses so that they can wail off more gallons of gas next weekend to get somewhere in time to get back again, etc. Fifteen miles of Camp Pendleton, and slow for the Immigration Checkpoint, where if you have olive skin, you have to pull over and speak to the officers. Past the nuclear plant that doesn't put out any watts. Past Church that doesn't have a church anymore. Past Lower Trestles

that doesn't have a trestle. Past Upper Trestles that does, and from the highway waves are visible, and it has glassed off. Then swing off the freeway, park and start the walk.

Pass three guys coming back at Uppers. "How's Lowers?" "Really good...really good...." "Anybody out?" "You're it...." Break into a run. Kind of a slate green evening. What Joyce called the snot-green sea, maybe, except with more grass in it. Clouds crowded down on the horizon. There would be wind in an hour or so.

Lowers was perfect. Six feet plus and back to its best for the first time in a year. Long, dark walls. Not a breath of a stir on the water. Not a soul on the sand; nobody else in the water. Just clouds above. Then paddling out for wave number six or eight or twenty or something, and the clouds broke apart above. They really did. There was a gigantic inner tube of cloud around Trestles, and up into the sky, except straight overhead. And overhead, planted straight in the center of the darkening blue, was a pockmarked moon. And right then, at that moment, two men were walking it. Alone at Trestles, the first trace of the wind dappling the surface, the waves perfect, after a day of exciting and great surfing, and there they were. So close. Nothing between us but 240,000 miles.

This slice of the 1968–69 North Shore season found SURFER editor Drew Kampion at his descriptive best.

Volume 10 | *Number 6*

LAST WINTER

BY DREW KAMPION

HALEIWA

A nice little town on the Kam Highway, just east of the bridge that (as bridges will) bridges the little river that flows out into Waialua Bay. Traveling east on Kam, right turn after the bridge and out to the point, splashing through deep, dark puddles, then lifting fine dust, then puddles again, along the side of the little harbor, out past the jetty and park. Haleiwa: nice place for kids to surf. Railroad tracks, ties, barbed wire and other rubbish rest in the silence amid the cauliflower-headed coral. A coral buttress rims the edge of the water. Waves come and break in the shallow water. Waves that are very steep on the takeoff, then grow steeper. Fast on the takeoff, they also grow faster. Often unescapable. Straightening off is the rule. Hang on. Sometimes, when it's fairly large, surfers straighten off, coast out in front of the face of the wave, only to have the thick, heavy, nasty lip hook out over them, landing with a thunderclap out ahead of the nose of their boards. The moment before that is a moment to consider. The day cut off, the eye going wide open for maximum light, the feeling of the atmosphere undergoing compression, being able to reach out, the moment here to hold, and touch the sinews and muscles that are coiled up in the underside of this dark wave. The moment when all possibilities are exhausted; when there are no alternatives, not even a good, decent panic; when there is nothing to do but divorce your mind from your body and watch the latter take a pounding. It is a deep moment, a quick moment, and, conceivably, a fatal moment. But it looks nice from the beach.

There is also some good fun that leads up to this moment. On this particular day, there were all kinds of people in the water. MacGillivray has talked Nat into surfing for pictures, and Nat is in the water, his left shoulder badly infected after an eventful prime merge with the bottom at Sunset. Ryan is out with Nat. Mark is back at Sunset and due anytime now. His hot-dog board fell off the car on the way over and now rests on the top of the car, good side up, Greg worrying about what Mark's going to say. Ron is using the thousands lens, his timing right on, smiling to himself, muttering "Haleiwa . . . Haleiwa. . . ." Greg's over at the tip of the point shooting right into the hold. Billy paddles out, and his kid is over helping Greg take movies. "Get lost . . . go see your mother. . . ." Dewey shows up with his hamburger hot-dog model, almost round like a garbage can lid. (Angie has his gun at Makaha.) Later, it proves too slow and skittish, as Dewey is overtaken and swallowed. Later still, off to the hospital for stitches on his forehead.

Jackie Baxter paddles out and pulls off some strong drives. Jimmy Lucas joins the crowd. Then Peter Johnson, Steve Bigler and Charlie Galanto sit in for a hand or two. Back from Makaha, quarter-pint-size Angie Reno makes it outside long enough to become an olive pit in one of the huge, hungry Haleiwa bowels. And Stoner chuckling to himself: "Haleiwa . . . Haleiwa. . . ."

NAT YOUNG
ANIMAL TRACKS AT HALEIWA
PHOTO: RON STONER

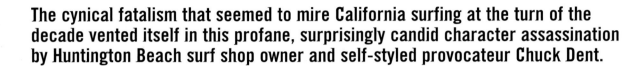

The cynical fatalism that seemed to mire California surfing at the turn of the decade vented itself in this profane, surprisingly candid character assassination by Huntington Beach surf shop owner and self-styled provocateur Chuck Dent.

Volume 10 | *Number 6*

BLOOD & SAND AT HUNTINGTON PIER

THIS ARTICLE RATED X

BY CHUCK DENT

Here I sit on Dead End Street, the original funky Broadway. The contest is over, and the almighty hawk is already blowing the sewage down the poverty pocket primrose lane. Only Lou Rawls could appreciate my position.

Beautiful downtown Huntington Beach: the seaside Peyton Place, the toilet, the asshole of the world. Also, my base of operations. I'm surrounded by Queebees, Okies, Afro-American Narcs, Geeks, Hippies, Earth Mothers, Roller Derby Lowriders, Air Watch Helicopters, Perverts, Degenerates, Space Cadets, Hardcore Animals, Pseudo-Surfers and the Establishment, the landlord waiting for urban renewal so the pier can be transformed into another plasticized mire like Tokyo, Sears and Disneyland; a place where the carney pitchmen pushing phony theories, basket-case superstars and ticky tack Fords and Chevys, instead of the Porsches and Ferraris they claim to produce (so-called surfboard manufacturers) can feel at Home Sweet Home.

My hemorrhoids are bleeding; have mercy on Fain for leaving me an extra tube of Preparation H (the fag bar in town ran out, which, incidentally, has become the rage, opening at 6 a.m.—fags in heat, patronized by virgin queens, gay blades and bull dikes . . . hurt me, hurt me). In formulating my own solution to the urgent problem of personal identity, I've become lost in this pit of paradox, this teeming melting pot.

Huntington Beach, the original Boy's Town, in the '30s a wide-open oil derrick, there were hookers hanging on roughnecks like cheap suits, gambling and vice that made Las Vegas look like Disneyland. Corruption was the standard of morality. Little Tijuana.

surfer
CDCE

Volume Eleven ■ Number One ■ March ■ $1.00

warning: this magazine contains sex, violence, dirty words, and sixty-foot disaster waves. may be harmful to anyone over 25.

LAST COVER OF THE DECADE
TOM STONE AT PIPELINE
PHOTO: ART BREWER

Chapter Two

The Seventies
Children of the Sea

By 1970, a year predicted by SURFER's slightly tripped-out editorial staff as "the end of the world," the magazine had more than a readership, it had a relationship. Its message mirrored the mood of its audience. The focused, inclusive content reflected changes that had taken place in the surfing world throughout the turbulent last days of the '60s. The commercialism that characterized the previous decade's heyday was now the poisoned doctrine of the Establishment; posing on surfboards was out, and total involvement with Mother Ocean was in. The shortboard revolution had weeded out the phonies, and it was a foregone conclusion that only true disciples could comprehend this bible. The cadre of SURFER editors, artists and photographers made sure these passionate feelings found a forum.

By this time, its founder, John Severson, had sold the magazine and followed his bliss to Maui. Kampion, perhaps the magazine's brightest comet, found his provocateur's ardor too hot not to cool down and eventually abdicated, leaving the mantle to be taken up by an unassuming Long Beach surfer named Steve Pezman. In 1971, Pezman took over as SURFER's editor and publisher and would deftly guide the publication for the next 20 years.

In many ways, Pezman had it easy right from the start. Not only was he working with some of the greatest talent in surf publishing—photographers like Steve Wilkings, Art Brewer, Jeff Divine, Craig Peterson and Warren Bolster, and writers like Kevin Naughton and Tom Morey—but he was also preaching to a congregation that had never in history been so united in its vision of itself. By the mid-1970s, surfers of the world looked alike, talked alike, thought alike. They all rode the same boards in primarily the same way and for primarily the same reasons. The entire surfing culture in 1974 shared an encompassing dream that manifested itself bimonthly, this fervent imagination fueled primarily by imagery of fantastic

surfers and fantasy surf—escape: the Zen of Gerry Lopez at Pipeline, the sojourns of Craig Peterson and Kevin Naughton throughout unexplored Africa and Central America, the myth of perfection, synthesized on the "Forgotten Island of Santosha" cover. SURFER in the mid-'70s was not so much a magazine as an article of faith. SURFER in 1964 told surfers what they were, SURFER in 1974 told them who they were.

And yet like everything else in this fluid medium, this mood was bound to change—and it did, in many ways as dramatically as during the late '60s conflagration. Surfing's Age of Aquarius lasted barely more than a half-dozen years. The idea that we surfed our way through life, straining for enough speed to make it through the Bowl of the Seventeen Lotus Blossoms made for fine romantic escapism, but by 1975, SURFER had seen the writing on the wall—because it was the wall.

In 1976, a new wave of commercialism began to swell. The growth of professional competitive surfing and the ensuing surf-industry boom marked the second half of the 1970s, and SURFER's role was subtly redefined. The magazine's publishing schedule went monthly in 1977. Surfers just couldn't get enough of this new self-actualized energy. With the emphasis on photography, taken to fabulous artistic heights by masters like Divine, Brewer, Craig Fineman and Australia's Peter Crawford, matched with insights from scribes like C.R. Stecyk, Neil Stebbins and Phil Jarratt, SURFER almost seamlessly made the jump from documentary to drama. Features delivered garish "Bronzed Aussie" profiles and coverage of the burgeoning professional competitive circuit with the same aplomb as they dished up epic images of modern fantasy islands like Bali and Nias. Ethics merged, and for the first time, soul and "sold out" somehow shared a page.

Drew Kampion assembled this cultural "time capsule" for SURFER's 1970 "End of the World" issue.

Volume 11 | *Number 2*

TIME CAPSULE: 1970

BY DREW KAMPION

Before the big mother strikes, we still have time to carefully place some of the more meaningful and sacred articles of our surfing culture into an indestructible time capsule. Maybe someday, some year, some one from Another World might uncover this capsule and come to know our world and our surfing before the Great Wave carried us into the backwash of extinction, beyond the reaches of cosmic consciousness. So take one long and last glance at these artifacts of an almost dead civilization, then turn bravely away to face the fate that awaits us all. All but One. . . .

CORKY CARROLL'S FIRST TROPHY
Corky has won more trophies in surfing contests than any other surfer. Therefore, this particular trophy has special relevance in this age of professionalism, antiprofessionalism and apathy.

CHUCK DENT'S DIAMOND RING
As the world spun toward its inevitable end, Chuck Dent sold the last of his oil wells, gave away his fleet of Porsches and fled to a monastery in South Bend, Indiana.

BIG SURF CRANK HANDLE
When this capsule turns up in the distant future, the discoverer can put two and two together, take this handle to Tempe, Arizona, and start the ball rolling . . . with a little bit of elbow grease, a lot of imagination and a craving for monetary gain.

MICKEY DORA'S DESK CALENDAR
Mickey predicted the Great Cataclysm for 1970 and, as usual, he hit the nail right on the head. Mickey's 1970 "Success" calendar goes into our time capsule fresh and unopened. Unfortunately, even Madagascar could not be saved.

A GOB OF TAR
Part of what made the last moments of the world worth remembering were the inspirational comments of oil company officials on the spread of their products throughout the world's beaches. Oil, for you curious, distant folks, was a substance refined at great expense in order to hasten the end of virtually everything good in the 1970 world.

PLANS FOR HONOLUA BAY HARBOR
These are the official Army Corps of Engineers plans for the granite-izing of Honolua Bay. Said a Corps official upon the release of the plans: "We don't have a harbor in the area, but we do have the funds. It'd be a nice place to park a boat, don't you think?" Perhaps the New World will take off where the ACE left off. Please don't.

A ROLL OF RECORDING TAPE (USED)
The uncut history of surfing by award-winning SURFER historian Sam Reid. Written during the last decade of the world, Sam's knack for writing simple, concise history, combined with his reputation as feature anthropologist of early surfing at SURFER Magazine, make this tape a natural for young and old. Running time: 73 weeks.

JOHN FAIN'S GUILD CARD
This is the card held by notable Hollywood performer Johnny Fain, who frequently backed up some of the western film capital's biggest stars. He always cherished those moments on the silver screen with Mickey Dora. Johnny also was a surfer, and he had a card for that, too, but he ripped it to shreds in frustration.

JOCK SUTHERLAND'S INDUCTION PAPERS
Jocko really did it. As history drew to an end in early 1970, Jock (long noted for putting himself in the worst possible situation in waves) put himself in to the worst possible situation in the world and joined the Army. Jeez!

A JOINT
A sample of Cannabis sativa, once a rare herb, which mysteriously blossomed almost everywhere in the late '60s. Its popularity cannot be explained. If the finder of the time capsule, however, is curious, he is welcome to try this sample.

GEORGE GREENOUGH'S GO-CART SPRING
The myth of George Greenough's insane go-cart driving has gotten completely out of hand. George doesn't have a go-cart. He doesn't drive it insanely through the back roads of Montecito. George likes to move slowly. But just to make sure, we're putting the throttle spring from his go-cart in the time capsule.

DEWEY WEBER'S FIRST DOLLAR
Once Dewey was a kid yo-yo champion on the street with holes in his pants. Now he's one of the biggest surfboard manufacturers in the world. He should remember his first dollar. He should also remember he still has holes in his pants.

A SURFER MAGAZINE
A highly sophisticated anthropological bimonthly publication that far outdistanced any magazine on the market in the early 1970s. The demise of this great publication, yea, institution, must be deemed as one of the greatest losses incurred during the period of cataclysm.

A ROLL OF INSTAMATIC FILM (EXPOSED)
The island of Maui is one of the greenest spots in the world. During the late '60s, it became a mecca for plant-hungry tourists looking for an all-time high in world travel. These photos are candids of WSA officials vacationing on Maui during the 1970 convention (which began sometime in 1965).

ROLL OF 16MM MOVIE FILM
This roll of film represents the supreme efforts of more than 4,062 motion-picture photographers. One frame from each surfing film ever made is spliced together. Included are the best frames from *Surf Safari*, *Cat on a Hot Foam Board*, *Surf's Up*, *Surf Psycho*, *The Endless Summer*, *Free and Easy*, *Evolution*, *Pacific Vibrations*, etc., etc., etc. The film runs an hour and a half. Also included: the best musical note from the score of each.

East Coast surfing's growing confidence was never so unabashedly expressed as in this "erotic confession" by Florida superstar Mike Tabeling.

Volume 11 | *Number 2*

I love Cocoa Beach

BY MIKE TABELING

I love you so tenderly; I love you hard. As one, you and I spend our days. You bring me pleasure; you bring me joy. The warmth of your waves and people makes me radiate from within. This glow I hope to express with words so all may understand.

It's true; I am in love with a town and its people. The town is Cocoa Beach and its adjoining boroughs. As for the people, I wish I could tell you about each one.

TIMMY NEWBERN
BLACKS BEACH
PHOTO: BRAD BARRETT

During the early '70s, the inherent joy of surfing took a backseat to what editor Drew Kampion saw as the much higher purpose of social change.

Volume 11 | Number 5

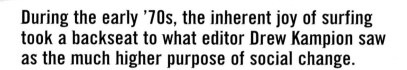

BY DREW KAMPION / ART BY RICK GRIFFIN

This is a desperate time. Everyone seeks a way out of, or a way into, their own minds. Their own places on Earth. We who read this magazine—look at it or make it up—all share a common knowledge: surfing. Whether there is anything else that identifies us with one another is either a matter of doubt or a matter of chance.

But because surfing is what we have in common, surfing is the medium through which we must communicate to each other, at least in the beginning. Later, we may find we share a love of nature, a desire for peace, a need for love, a common friend or a particular belief. But first, because this is a surfing magazine, and because this is the place where we all meet, first we have surfing.

And that is why, when the world is the way it is and the future is the way it is and we are the way we are, we still speak of surfing. It's like the weather. In a time of alienation and fear and doubt, the rain falls on us all and the sun shines on everyone.

It is only that which makes what follows valid or of interest. And if it makes no sense and wanders, so what? It's just words about something we have in common.

I knew at those honest-with-myself moments that 1970 was going to be a critical year, especially for surfing. Mickey Dora had gone to the trouble of making up a graph that showed plummeting cataclysm right where 1970 was, and I know damn well that Mickey wouldn't make such an effort had he not received some highly pertinent information from headquarters.

But we all know how it is with doom forecasts: we neglect them/laugh at them/disbelieve them because that is how we want to see them. But this time, there appears to be something heavy blowing in the wind. Not the end of the world, perhaps (that will come soon enough, our scientists say, even if we don't budge an inch), but certainly the end of something. Call it an era maybe.

In California, a curse is upon the coast. Each year, the surf grows grayer; each year, each classic surf spot grows a little worse. The water sloshes lethargically off the cluttered beaches. Gobs of oil still dip and sway with the tidal surges. Kelp dies and lets the wind in, or chokes what waves there are. The California sea seems eternally leaden. Void of that bubbly, sudsy, salty quality so attractive in Hawaiian and Australian surf.

Still, it seems there is no call for alarm. Rather, it has passed that stage already. Man continues to disrupt the natural order of things. The peace and love constituencies shift their allegiances to violence and hate. Even now there is no appreciable indication of any shift from man's present entrenchment in a totally materialistic, product-oriented society. Our outward progress is so far outrunning our inward (metaphysical) progress that the only result can be a mankind living in a totally mechanized and unwieldy civilization that he cannot begin to understand or control. This in turn will produce an unprecedented chaos, like an infant behind the wheel of a sophisticated luxury car.

And if you're a California (or non-California) surfer, what do you do?

It seems to me that surfing by itself is clean and basic and real enough to transcend this era of anarchy and unrest. Because surfing, in its pure form, deals with an equilibrium involvement between man and his nature, it becomes, almost by definition, an ecologically pure undertaking. Perhaps even an undertaking so basic that it performs an evolutionary function.

But this, too, is the cause of Mickey Dora's cataclysmic forecast. Good and bad cannot long dwell in the same house. One will be driven out.

It is surfing's good fortune to be driving out the bad. Exploitation of surfing is on the wane. It will be replaced again by the basic unit of this natural bond between man and wave: surfing.

Because when wars and flags and religions and nations and cities and rockets and taxicabs and monosodium glutamate and television are gone, there will still be an order to things far beyond the order of power-crazed men. It will be the order of a universe at equilibrium with all natural forces in balance.

And that is what riding a wave is.

HOW ARE DANGER AND FEAR RELEVANT TO YOUR SURFING?

Danger and fear in a lot of cases are direct stimuli and push for you to understand more fully the situation. Danger is constituted as a situation where you might get some bodily harm done to you, whereas fear, I think, is in the area of mental harm, like paranoia or ignorance of a situation. But danger and fear combined are both territorial aspects of your involvement, which can be overridden by understanding. You have a greater fear beyond the territory that you're accustomed to, for sure, because you're ignorant; you don't know what's happening with the situation. But as far as danger is concerned, that's a thing separate from your own fear, although it's sometimes supplemented by fear.

SO DANGER IS OBJECTIVE AND FEAR IS SUBJECTIVE?

Right, although the subjectiveness of fear can supplement the objectiveness of danger.

THERE'S A STORY AROUND ABOUT HOW YOU SURFED 25-FOOT WAIMEA LAST WINTER AND GOT CAUGHT OUT AFTER DARK. WAS THERE ANY FEAR GOING ON IN ALL OF THAT?

No, it was mostly just danger.

NOT TOO MUCH FEAR?

Well, on the other hand [laughs], maybe it was mostly fear and not any danger. Actually, the way I felt was that danger was secondary to fear. I didn't feel there was any danger of me getting injured or anything. I might have thought I was gonna get killed. I got caught inside and wasn't watching the outside indicators and lamed out, just got sucked in. I tried to catch a smaller wave and missed it and turned around and there was this big set coming. I didn't make it, even after some furious scratching. Righteously broke a good board, too!

WHAT MADE YOU GO OUT THAT NIGHT?

Oh, just to get some refreshing waves before dark. Everybody'd split, though, so I thought, well, it's gonna have to be kind of a lone wolf thing. Gonna have to get out there and earlobe over the whole thing. I got about five or six waves before I broke the board. Pretty decent 18- to 20-foot waves. Y'know, drop in, glide for a while,

kick out. Or heavy left rail down into the maul for a good turn, then pull out. I wasn't trying to be too creative. Just an evening go-out.

DO YOU PREFER BIG WAVES OR SMALLER WAVES? AND WHERE?

I like the fair-to-middling 8- to 10-foot waves best. Anywhere. The Trestle on a good day is keen for drawing long lines or for elevators, whereas the Pipe or an 8- or 10-foot day is keen for getting in the tube and doing really clean maneuvers.

HOW 'BOUT THAT TUBE?

The tube at the Pipe is a very clean divider. The tube at the Pipe is just like an ax. You either make it or you don't. If you do make it, then you have all kinds of various and sundry other places wherein you can make it, such as up to the curl or back around or straight down the line for a hundred yards, then back up into the white water for an el rollo. But if you don't make it, then it seems like there's only one direction to go, and that's to protect your life from getting snuffed out on the bottom or obliterated by some rambunctious coral head. Cantankerous coral head, I should say.

WHAT ABOUT THE WAVE THAT'S IN PACIFIC VIBRATIONS WHERE YOU SPEND QUITE A BIT OF TIME IN THE TUBE?

It was all right. I knew it was kind of a fat situation before I took off because earlier waves had been walling up in a similar manner, but when I dropped in, I didn't realize it was gonna happen like that ahead of me, as quick as it did. So what I did was almost automatic. When I hit the bottom, I had to pull it off quickly 'cause I watched the fringe and saw what it was doing. I had to pull up into it as fast as I could, instead of drawing off a long turn. I saw that there was no other way to make the wave except to pull up tight into it, knowing the Pipe as I do. There's a heavy margin of error as far as being in the tube. That, plus the fact that I was perhaps dissatisfied with several of my previous rides.

WAS THERE A LOT OF ROOM INSIDE?

Spacious for sure. Just like the Pope's living room. Even with all the bric-a-brac, paintings and big overstuffed chairs and sofas, there was still a lot of room inside of the thing.

IS BEING IN THE POPE'S LIVING ROOM AS BIG A CHARGE AS, SAY, RIDING THOSE EVENING WAVES AT WAIMEA?

Maybe more so, but it's hard to say. You can't say that riding in a tube is necessarily better than riding big waves. They're on similar planes; they're all coming from the same airport, so to speak. You can get blown out by riding a big wave, and you can get blown out by riding in a tube. But I would say in direct comparison that riding back in the tube at Pipe is a more enlightening occurrence.

Winner of the SURFER Poll as the top surfer of 1970, Hawaii's Jock Sutherland exuded a weird eloquence—especially when talking about the tube.

Volume 11 | Number 6

IN THE POPE'S LIVING ROOM WITH JOCK SUTHERLAND

BY DREW KAMPION

JOCK SUTHERLAND
LAYING IT DOWN AT PIPE
PHOTO: ART BREWER

Surfer designer/innovator/inventor and notable freethinker Tom Morey penned this physio-philosophical treatise just before he began development of the flexible "boogie" board.

Volume 12 | *Number 2*

Surfing Waves

BY TOM MOREY

Surfing, working, playing, skiing, boxing, sleeping, loving . . . a lot of names have been used in an attempt to describe and to categorize an activity that is continuous, smooth, fluid and graceful—generally known as living. Life comes forth and is seen and evaluated for opportunity. The liver positions himself as best as he can (after pushing through a lecture from Dad, three bullies at the corner, dog shit on the bottom stair), then the opportunities come; he picks one he thinks he can handle and rides it out.

Good or poor ride? Depends on how skillful the rider is.

Isn't it all surfing, really? Doesn't one surf his way through the waves of traffic up the highway through the thought waves racing through his head, the waves of music blaring from his stereo, to a movie? Isn't a candy bar an easy ride? A man-made wave of calculated sweetness? The taking off of the wrapper, the climbing and dropping of your jaws, the deliciousness of the inside, the energy contained within it, transferred to you giving you motion? The apparentness of there being something in the beginning and it being gone at the end?

And what about making love . . . and mowing the lawn and not bogging the motor to a halt in deep grass . . . surfing your razor through your beard every morning and trying to never cut your face . . . laying drums in a "rock and roll" band . . . writing a term paper or a book report on a book you've not really read (how well can you ride a new spot without spending some time "reading" where the lineup is, the effects of tide change, wind conditions, who's a hazard out there, who is too aggressive to handle . . . all that). Or . . . picture yourself reading a book . . . reading your way through someone's brain prints . . . head tracks. You're rolling along fine, then suddenly get stalled out on some hard-looking word or phrase that you're not used to . . . getting lost and not being able to recover . . . not being able to keep up with the curl . . . a word like "aspartylphenylalanine" forms unexpectedly in your path like some weird little choppy section.

Talking with someone. Now there's a surfing activity if ever there was one. Two waves of oceans communicating to each other . . . whew! How easy is it to get bored with the other guy's rap and shoot him a "yeah, far out"? And how easy is it to bore someone else and take his "yeah, far out" as a genuine, for-real comment? He's talking. You wait for just the right time, stalling, stalling, nodding and nodding, smiling, then the lineup is there for you—the opening comes (now!); you drop in carefully with a "yeah, like, you know . . . " and move forward onto your point . . . not too much weight here or emphasis there, a little more now, there . . . easy on the pressure; don't blow your position. A few more words then cut back, "then, on the other hand. . . . " You rap off a couple more strong turns then whiiii-ick and out over the top, clean. Paddle your way through two or twenty of his thoughts; watch how they form, the intensity of each . . . size it all up. Learn from him just as you learn by reading the tumbling soup and the spilling heaps of blue-green wobble that we've all come to love.

JERICHO POPPLER
DANCE FORM FOR A LIQUID STAGE
PHOTO: JEFF DIVINE

Australian filmmaker Paul Witzig (Evolution, Sea of Joy) offered this naive, optimistic solution to the world's problems.

Volume 12 | Number 3

WHEN EVERYONE SURFS

BY PAUL WITZIG

My main aim in making this new film is to turn people on to surfing. And if I concentrate mainly on younger audiences, it is because I want to make films for the children of this world. If we are to have any hope for the future, it rests with the children and not with the older people—mostly totally conditioned and set in their ways, accepting the hideous state of world affairs as normal, neither wanting nor working for a world of peace, brotherhood and love.

Surfers are a new race. I'd like to fully convert them to a free surfing life before society takes them and molds them into cannon fodder or some other role our elders have chosen for youth. You see, our world really is a totally beautiful place. It is only man who works to destroy this paradise. Instead of searching for truth and beauty, he worships power and money. So, of all men, the surfer, almost alone, strives to live in harmony with nature and the world around him. This the sea teaches him, and he asks for no more—because he receives everything.

If I have a message, this is it: that in a pure surfing life, man can reach a level of physical, mental and spiritual harmony. Waves are part of nature's bounteous gift to man. To ride beautiful waves, or to watch gifted surfers, is to partake in, or witness, a truly creative event. I cannot physically take the audience out into the water, but I can capture their minds and take them with me to many wondrous places. Where fantastic, beautiful, powerful, clean and mellow waves break on palm-fringed reefs and beaches.

You can be free if you want to be. The world is a big and beautiful place, just waiting for you. Surf is everywhere—many strange and wondrous places to beckon and bewitch you. Many new friends to meet and to play with. Many waves to ride, many experiences to share, much love to be given and to receive.

This is my life and the life of my friends. We want everyone to do it. When everyone does it, there will be no time for wars and killing, no time for stupid rules made by stupid old men. Everyone will be too busy surfing and getting it on. I am not really trying to say that surfing is a cure for all the world's ills. But through music, through films and in lots of other ways, we are trying to get you to realize that you are free to live the way you want to, free to discover that big, beautiful, alive world of which surfing is but a part.

JOEY CABELL
FIFTH GEAR AT SUNSET BEACH
PHOTO: ART BREWER

NEWPORT BEACH
*"STYLE IS THE
MAN HIMSELF"*
PHOTO: ART BREWER

Kampion again, attempting, by his own account, "to put into words what can really only be truly expressed with a beastlike howl."

Volume 12 | *Number 5*

STYLE

BY DREW KAMPION / ART BY RICK GRIFFIN

I know that Joey Cabell is great, but I do not understand why, really. I have a feeling of inadequacy while watching him surf large waves. A feeling that a mind capable of handling such a huge, rushing mass of chaos in such an orderly, efficient manner must be light-years ahead of my training-wheel reality.

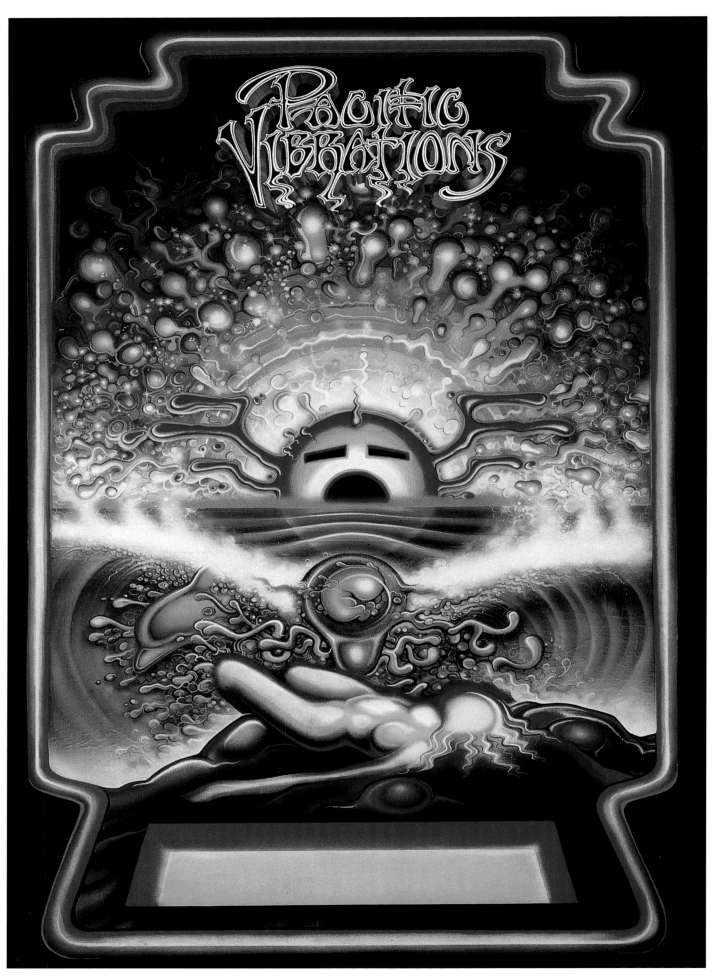

RICK GRIFFIN'S *PACIFIC VIBRATIONS* **POSTER, CIRCA 1970**
JOHN SEVERSON'S LAST FILM CAPTURED A TIME IN SPACE

RANDY PIDD
PRE-SUBDIVISION RIGHTS AND LEFTS
PHOTO: JEFF DIVINE

"What we're doing is creating a controlled atmosphere on the Ranch, and keeping it basically agriculture and cattle. We've formed a Ranch owners' association, and all the parcel owners will be in the association. They actually will control the Ranch when we've finished selling the parcels. We've survey-staked and monumented all of the Ranch into parcels of 100 acres or larger. At this point, we have more than 1,900 acres of 'common areas.' All of the beach is common area to all owners.

It's not a development in any way. We're not building any golf courses, and I don't see that it will become a country club atmosphere at all—the people just don't want it. It's just strictly a ranch that's being divided, and will be totally operated as a ranch. In order to keep it that way, we have a security force. These men are all deputized by the County of Santa Barbara, and will strictly enforce the trespass laws. The Ranch is only for the owners and their guests, period! There just isn't anyone else that will be allowed on the Ranch. I might stay on that for just a minute because, in the past, due to articles in your magazine and because of just word-of-mouth and the previous lack of security on the Ranch, a lot of surfers have come in, walked in and whatnot to surf the beaches and I'd like to get the message across to these people that the Ranch is closed. We operate under the law and with the law. And now that the railroad has given us permission to patrol their tracks, there just isn't going to be a way to get in here. We're not here to hassle the kids or to give them a bad time, but we are going to protect our rights and keep everyone off the Ranch, except owners and guests. We have had a policy of warning a first time, and the second time they are caught, we have them arrested and prosecute them to the limit of the law. The judge they go before is a judge in the local area here, and is agrarian oriented, and he's also a property owner here. The boys are not getting off with light fines; they're getting the maximum fines—I believe it's $125 the first time out, and then I believe it's $500 and five days the second time. Again, the purpose of this security group is not to hassle the surfers but to protect our rights. We have pretty well defined the mean high-tide line as being the wet-sand area, and the judge has gone along with it. It's really sort of unfortunate that these surfing beaches are not down in some public area, but from what the surfers tell me, if they were, it would get so crowded they wouldn't be any good anyway." — *DICK LaRUE*

The ultimate SURFER scam, surf and photo access for this feature was granted by real estate developers of the newly subdivided Hollister Ranch in return for running this blatant, but ultimately successful sales pitch.

Volume 13 | Number 2
RANCH REALITY

A short south-of-the-border paean, written by Mexico-run regular Steve Pezman.

Volume 13 | Number 6

MEXICO

BY STEVE PEZMAN / ART BY RICK GRIFFIN

The minute you cross the border into Mexico, a very real sense of adventure and discovery prevails. Even for those who have journeyed south many times, the changes of vibes are obvious. The road now has potholes; a question asked in English gets a quizzical stare, and who knows, as the sun goes down, what the coming dawn will bring?

For surfers in a car loaded with supplies and boards, the possibilities are endless. Should we stop in that interesting looking cantina over there and shoot down a few cervezas, or maybe power on and try to make Mazatlan before dark? And then days, weeks and months begin to intermix, time becomes abstracted, and animal instincts take over. Hunger—let's eat. Thirst—let's drink! Waves—let's find some! Lazy—perfect, let's just lay here. Endless numbers of little dirt roads wander off the main road heading for the coast. Each one poses a possibility; there could be waves down there. And so, with no pressures or tasks other than what whims dictate, you turn off and head across fields of corn hacked out of the jungle and wind up into the mountains covered with banana groves, and the road turns into a 2 mph streambed gorge, and then the wheel tracks pick up again, move through a dense rain forest around another curve, and suddenly there's the ocean, a small fishing village, a river . . . and out there at the boulder-strewn mouth of the river, the kind of soul-stirring sight that makes surfers head south.

Escapism was the obvious message in this clever fiction piece dealing with how far a surfer would go for a few uncrowded waves.

Volume 14 | Number 1

NO OBSERVABLE PROGRESS

BY ALVIN DARKLING

It was raining and there was nothing to do. Outside his small apartment, across the slick concrete of the Coast Highway, lay the beach. Beyond the sand, the ocean was moving about nervously, the waves so helplessly confused that not even a solitary rider had ventured out for a surf.

He knew that as soon as the storm passed and the waves cleaned up a touch, there would be several hundred people out scratching for every riplet. This knowledge did nothing to improve the rather negative mood he had fallen into. He was also scared. It was a fear that had been lingering somewhere within him for several years. It was a fear that had grown familiar, a fear of never being able to be alone with the waves again.

At first he had traveled.

The Islands. Fifty guys out at Honolua at the first sign of a swell pouring through the Molokai Channel. France. Crowds at La Fintenia, an international scene at Hossegor. Crowds in Barbados, crowds at Jeffreys, always crowds, and his money had run out. Now California was home again, and it was raining, and he was bored.

He picked up yesterday's newspaper off the floor to see what was playing at the 75-cent movie house. Hoping for a place to invest his energy for a couple of hours.

He never got to the film section, for on page six of the day-old paper, he found his future. Tucked away between an airline hijacking and a dope bust was a headline that nailed his attention to the stale print:

STATE TO PURCHASE SUNRISE HILLS BEACH PROPERTY
PLANS CALL FOR CONSTRUCTION OF MENTAL INSTITUTION

Into his mind flashed sea and sky-colored memories of magical days at Sunrise Hills, riding the waves that broke so perfectly upon the reefs there. Sure it was a couple of hours' drive, and you had to sneak in because it was private property, but, damn, when the spot was doing it, any hassle was worthwhile. And now the state wanted the beach. Damn! Closing his eyes softly allowed him to see the hot, clean tubular right that he loved; the mental picture was so vivid and real that he could not imagine being denied access to these waves. But there it was in black and white.

He began to read the article, with sadness altering his perception at first.

"Secretary of Finance, Jensen Cutino, today announced that the state has purchased 10 acres of land in the Sunrise Hills area. This acreage includes the South Beach section of Sunrise Hills."

TIM LYNCH
LA JOLLA SHORES
PHOTO: JEFF DIVINE

Merely the premier spot. Smokes on low tide, playful on high.

"Cutino stated that an ultra-modern facility for the treatment of the mentally disturbed would be built on the land."

Wonderful. An insane asylum overlooking one of the hottest waves on the coast. He read on through a few statistics: cost of construction, projected number of patients, etc., and then he came to the final paragraph. A paragraph that changed his life.

"Dr. Harold Gardner, who has been appointed chief of staff for the new institution, has these words of assurance for homeowners in the surrounding area: 'We plan to keep the institution totally secluded. That is why we have purchased so much land. Aside from the high therapeutic effect on our patients, we can also be quite sure that no one will be wandering in or out of the area.'"

Totally secluded.

The next morning, the weather cleared, but he did not surf. Instead, he went to the library and checked out a copy of *The Divided Personality*. And during the next year, he read every volume on personality disorder he could find. And during the next year, the Sunrise Hills Institution for the Mentally Disturbed rose quietly upon the green hillside overlooking the rather perfect waves that snapped over the reefs of South Beach.

No one surfed there anymore. One thousand-dollar fine and up to two years in jail for trespassing on state land. Penalties so severe that no fence was necessary, just a few highly visible signs by the highway.

The institution officially opened on April 1. On April 2, he ordered a new board from the shop. A reef-break stick. It was ready in a few days. The board felt pure and almost magical in his hands. Quite carefully, he placed it in the racks of his old Bug and drove up the coast toward Sunrise Hills.

PATIENT ADMISSION REPORT

Patient approached front gate naked, carrying a surfboard under his arm. In a coherent manner, patient announced that he was a member of the "Yeti People."

Patient announced that he had traveled here from his hometown in the Himalaya Mountains by "translocation" (apparently a form of mental travel). Patient mentioned that he had come to claim the hospital and surrounding property in the name of the rightful owners, "the Yeti People."

He was placed in a "harmless" ward, and thus had beach-going privileges. He convinced the doctors that surfing was relaxing to him. And the aide/lifeguard kept an eye on him to make sure he didn't start to paddle for Catalina.

The surf was excellent all spring.

PATIENT REVIEW: ONE YEAR IN INSTITUTION

Patient spends most of his time alone in the ocean. At night, patient can be heard giggling and laughing for no apparent reason. Still claims to be from the Himalaya. Patient is making no observable progress toward reality.

He had his own small room. His neighbors were, respectively, Mr. Lazlo, who thought he was a pigeon and spent all day cooing, and Leon. Leon was God.

"I am God. Welcome to this place. Do you like old cowboy shows? I am God," said Leon when they met.

When there was no surf, he meditated or did yoga on the cliff high above the blue-green sea. Time passed by in dreamlike fashion. Summer brought south-swell perfection.

One afternoon, Lazlo was released. He promised to stay in touch by "pigeon mail." Lately, Leon had decided he was Brett Maverick, TV cowboy star.

THIRD-YEAR PATIENT REVIEW

Patient still claims to be a "righteously idealed Yeti personage." Says the crown prince of Belgium and the Dalai Lama have sworn him to secrecy over the mission he is on. Patient is making no observable progress toward reality.

He was alone in his own wonderful daydream, with a lifetime of sparkling multicolored wave faces to dance upon. It was, he thought with a smile, "unreal."

One of the most influential SURFER articles ever published; Larry Yates' film tie-in feature on the Indian Ocean island of Mauritius redefined the Myth of Perfection, triggering a restless search for Nirvana that continues to this day.

Volume 15 | Number 1

FORGOTTEN ISLAND OF SANTOSHA

BY LARRY YATES

WHAT LED YOU THERE?

It was a place that we had discovered on a previous trip. Just something you'd heard about maybe, but never been to. I was there for about half a year the first time.

AND THIS WAS A RETURN . . .

Yes. A return to capture it on film.

I lived in a thatched, tin-roof house on the tip of the bay. It had a bathroom and kitchen, very native and functional. I could walk out my front gate right to the edge of the water. When the surf came up, my room on the bay would just echo and sing with the sound of the waves. As a group, we had three different houses. A house for the photographers so they could work in peace, and so we could live in peace. Rent was very cheap. We all saw each other every day to go surfing and do other things. The beaches there are beautiful, untouched, pure white coral sand. You could find shells the size of your forearm. It was like you'd imagine Hawaii to have been 50 years ago.

But here on Santosha, there seems no measure for time. Toward the end of that warm winter season, we experienced a swell that defies description with mere words. She showed us her full beauty and intensity. We felt we could not ask for more.

Santosha really isn't a place; it's a word. It just has a meaning. It's a state of mind. A forgotten state of mind.

LARRY YATES
DRAWING DREAM LINES IN "SANTOSHA"

U.S. CHAMPS
TEXAS, 1975
PHOTO: RUSS CALISCH

The definitive surfing sartorial statement by Steve Pezman.

Volume 15 | Number 2

SOMETHING YOU PUT ON TO GO NAKED IN

BY STEVE PEZMAN

A good pair of trunks are like two-year-old Levi's. They know where you are, and you know where they are . . . a little insolently hanging off, but not coming off. Loose in the leg so they don't bind when you sit on your board. Fastened at the top correctly, too. You can get wax out of the pocket and back in a hurry. And for some reason, you don't lose this pair or someone doesn't rip them off . . . Until one day, finally, after a couple of summers and a winter or two, they just give out in the crotch, but you stay out anyway. And you take them home that night to have your girlfriend fix 'em. But she tells you they're dusted, and you figure you just have to get a new pair.

Associate editor Kurt Ledterman gave his penchant for eroticizing surf spots' free reign in this torrid stanza.

Volume 15 | Number 2

MS. PIPELINE POEM

The Pipeline has the power
over those who dare to ride her.
To get them in positions
that lead to end of slide,
straighten out into a waterfall,
or dive and scratch for deepness.
Paddle hard to push the lip
in vain, because of steepness.
Three moments for war stories
told later when fear subsides
about the rush, about the tube,
about her all-time rides . . .
'cause like all women she's just insane.
— *ARCHISABBA*

"THREE MOMENTS FOR WAR STORIES . . . "
PHOTO: JEFF DIVINE

This was the high point of Kevin Naughton's and Craig Peterson's 1975 travel series, chronicling serendipitous turns of fortune on the global surf trail.

TITO ROSENBERG AND KEVIN NAUGHTON
SAHARAN NIGHTS
PHOTO: CRAIG PETERSON

Volume 16 | Number 2

BENEATH THE AFRICAN SUN

BY CRAIG PETERSON AND KEVIN NAUGHTON

Our beach camp was adjacent to the bluffs. This was a good move, as we found out later, because at night large scorpions emerge from the bluff and seek a source of warmth (i.e., the human body). Scorpion bites in these parts can incapacitate a person anywhere from two days to two weeks, depending on the type of scorpion. Beaches are one of the only places that scorpions won't traverse.

The air was dry, and there was no problem with mosquitoes, so we slept out under the stars. On clear nights when millions of stars provide a moving light show, talk comes easy on almost every subject under and above the sky; folks, friends, girls (past, present and hopefuls), scams, shooting stars, state of surfing, music, places we're going to, places we've been, sins, dreams, life history, philosophizing, surf, religion, people, ambitions, failures and the more mysterious—UFOs, witchcraft, devil's triangles, supernatural and other inexhaustible subjects, such as sleeping (pun intended).

After waking, we showered ourselves in the waves on the tail end of a 2- to 3-meter swell. We were in the water long enough to get it wired, but not long enough to surf out. The swell dissipated by that afternoon. That's when the hardships started. With no swell and not much to do but wait for another one by ourselves, our problem was staying healthy, safe and occu-pied. Kevin pored over books with a speed-reader's intensity, and Craig chained his camera case to anything that didn't move. Our diet amounted to basic blandness: bread, canned sardines, cheese, nuts and fruit—break-fast and dinner. Every nook and cranny in our vicinity was inspected. We kept an unrelenting watch on our gear, as the area we were in is infamous for thievery. One unfortunate guy we met had been sleeping in his van with friends one night when local brigands with a container of sleeping gas slipped a hose through the top ventilation opening in the front window and gassed the inside of the car. The guy woke up a day later with a splitting headache and a ransacked auto; almost everything was gone. Naturally, we were a bit disconcerted by this and other stories, and likewise took precau-tions with our gear. We fortressed our tiny camp each evening as though we were preparing for the siege of Khartoum. Still, it was uncomfortable sleep-ing with all our possessions under, around and on top of us. Then to wake up in the morning in a sand pit formed by thrashing dreams of being buried alive in the middle of the Kalahari.

An insufferable heat made our clothes feel like burlap, and no nearby abundant supply of freshwater meant a bath was out of the question. It was difficult finding an adequate supply of drinking water. Hot sun, little shade and no waves after five days of waiting in this condition made our predicament seem hopeless.

Hopeless, that is, until we met Tito.

LOG TWO

The dust-brown Land Rover rumbled to a halt near our piled-up gear. Out stepped a short guy with frizzled black hair and a grizzled beard. His whole face smiled warmly as he surveyed the scenery and finally us. He wore old Levi's, a red plaid Pendleton and hiking boots, and had the cut of a misplaced lumberjack. Craig smiled back and Kevin grimaced through cracked lips.

"Hey, how you guys doing? Looks nice here. Waves been any good lately?" he asked in an accent we couldn't place.

"It's picked up a bit today. Good a few days ago, maybe tomorrow," Kevin replied hoarsely.

He took a close look at our haggard features like he was sizing us up.

"Man, you guys look like you're in poor shape. You just cross the desert or something?" He wiped his brow and looked up as if to find the heat that was bearing in from all sides. "It's too hot out here. You want to step inside and munch some tangerines?"

"Sure!" Craig plodded to the car with the stamina of a man who had just chased a mirage. Kevin lagged close behind.

Once inside the car, our situation felt better. The owner extracted a bag of tangerines from a refrigerator and offered us all we could eat. He looked American, but the accent had a Latin touch.

"Where you from?" we asked.

"Brazil! I've come over here from Brazil to travel all around Africa and ride some 'tooobes!' My name's Tito."

"Brazil! All right! You're the first Brazilian surfer we've ever met! We're from California."

"That's OK, I won't hold it against you guys."

Laughter, more talk and tangerines.

"…you guys are hitchhiking! That must be difficult here."

"Yeah," said Kevin, wistfully, as he eyed the roomy interior of the Rover. "But we haven't had any choice."

There was a moment's pause.

"Well, why don't you guys join up with me for a while? I've been traveling alone, and the three of us could share the costs. This car will go anywhere!"

Our jackpot eyes were sufficient replies to Tito's offer. Thus began three weeks of African surf exploration in a new Land Rover with a Brazilian surfer/traveler.

We passed the remainder of the day becoming better acquainted with each other. Tito personified the finer qualities of the Latin people: warm, open, garrulous, enthusiastic and overly friendly. The type of personality that lingers in your mind long after the image fades.

His car was a remarkable fully equipped surf vehicle: stove, fridge, sink, sand ladders, winch, tape deck, bed, reduction box, spotlights, tent, roof racks, double locks, etc.

"What don't you have in this car?" Craig asked, incredulously.

"She split back home a month ago," replied Tito.

FROM LEFT: KEVIN NAUGHTON AND DAVE TERRY
LIBERIA
PHOTO: CRAIG PETERSON

KEVIN NAUGHTON
SPANISH SAHARA
PHOTO: CRAIG PETERSON

Senior SURFER photographer Art Brewer, as expressive on the page as behind the camera, mused on the fragile nature of surf sanctuaries.

Volume 16 | Number 5

ALL OTHER PLACES

BY ART BREWER

The fungus is growing.

Overcrowded surfing spots. Many turned into harbors as man pushes forward.

Flashback:

Approximate time: say 30 hours back, or is it 40 years? Driving south on a national highway over the hills (through a valley of flowers) to a bay somewhere in the Indian Ocean on one of the southern tips of the world.

From the road, you can see waves, long lines of waves undulating in perfect unison, three-quarters of a mile in length. Almost geometrical in their symmetry. Rub your eyes! Pinch yourself! Is it real?

It's what you'd think California would be like in the 1920s or '30s. Except it's happening now, and it's a perfect wave that pushes into a large bay where the whales mate and porpoises patrol the point.

It was real! It was perfect! The best right. Six to 8 feet for eight days. Breaking on three different points that are strung together by those long walls.

Waves averaged 250 yards right down the line. For the masters, some waves were three-quarters of a mile long. The masters were the connectors.

At this place, it is said that Nat Young rode from the outermost corner. The ride being approximately 1 mile in length, maybe more. An 8- to 10-foot wave that took him four minutes to ride to the beach where he finally stepped off on the sand to lay down and rest.

But this time it was an international congregation of surfing talents, amongst them Terry Fitzgerald, who rode this bay for three days (three perfect days) 6 to 8 feet, during which time he caught the three most perfect waves of the three days. His surfing was quick, with smooth, controlled speed—sly—moving forward even when turning back—weightless but controlled at all times. Cleanly—a master of his craft. One of his waves was timed at 120 seconds before we lost sight of him. A half hour later, he could be seen walking back up to the paddle-out spot. At the end of the third day, Fitz left, asking, "What more can I do?" while others stayed to try and answer that question for themselves.

The village is one and a half miles from the takeoff spot, a peaceful fishing village that mail from Hawaii takes three to four weeks to reach. One market, two fish-and-chips shops and a hardware store. Fish and chips are 40 cents, whole-wheat bread, 18 cents; other items match. Also three small hotels. The setting, early California 1920s or '30s. It's winter and most homes have no heating. It's a cold run to the outhouse in the morning.

Here the sun rises over the ocean. Waking the first morning and looking out my window, I saw a place black people call "clay reef" and white people call "windows"…looking long and strung out just across Daiz Road in front of Peter Daniels' house. We surfed this green-blue backlit tubing wave for an hour and a half just to warm up for the real thing: "The Bay." Many mornings were spent watching the sunrise and "window" waves out the front door of Peter's house.

The dune used to peak high and run to the shells along water's edge. But now, 'dozers cut down the sand dunes along the bay for houses and parking. We will flash on the good times and what they were then and how a world of our own creation is closing in on all other places.

TERRY FITZGERALD
THE SULTAN OF SPEED, JEFFREYS BAY, SOUTH AFRICA
PHOTO: ART BREWER

SURFER gave an evocative name to the 1975 summer south swell against which all others have been measured since.

Volume 16 | Number 5

MONSTER FROM NEW ZEALAND

BY RICHARD SAFADY

The coastal cruise included 10-footers at the big T (Trestles) in Marineland, Cottons, Newport Point and the Wedge, as usual, and back breakers off the bottoms of the Huntington and Manhattan Beach piers. Beaches from Venice north to Will Rogers were closed to all but experienced swimmers because of dangerous rips. More than 440 rescues were made. By 10 a.m. Thursday morning, while driving by Santa Monica, you could tell this was going to be the highest surf in years. Further north to Sunset, Chart House, then Topanga, all the Malibu indicators kept pulling you onward like a magnet. Because of the high tides, it was sandbag time for some of the beachfront houses. It reminded me of the Chambers Bros. song, "People get ready, there's a change a comin'." Approaching Malibu, the parking problem was just that. But you gotta drive by just to see this place. Yep, it's hard to go any farther. The 50-cent lot is full. You get it done, though, and once on the beach, you know it's gonna be show time. All three points are being heavily surfed. Looking around as you walk up to the points: the sand display resembles the *Sgt. Pepper's* album cover. Back-to-school attendance must be way off. The shorebreak was eating away the beach north of the pier. The sand beach drop-off of carried-away sand is a wall 30 yards long, up to 6 feet high. Inside point at medium-high tide is a fatter wave, lots of water, sloping bottom. Medium tide starts to round out the bottom, connecting the middle and outside point. Goofyfoots Mark Johnson and Bobby Warchola put on a rare show and tell. Midday and still no wind. San Blas hot. Ten-footers at third, lots of 8 and 9ers, fast angle riding. Tide dropping, less bottom turning, faster sections. Guards Baker, Craig, Hoberg, Lefay and Stevenson were keepin' busy. Some calling it the best. Weber going back to '66 for comparison. People are returning with faster, longer boards than they had arrived with earlier in the day. Inside it's 7 feet on the sets. Waves almost to the pier. Accidents a plenty. The usual comments are heard. And some new ones. I was told I'm on Patty Hearst's death list. That's the vibe at the "'Bu."

CROSSTOWN TRAFFIC AT THE 'BU
PHOTO: RAY ALLEN

Written under a pen name, Craig Stecyk's subversive and ultimately cynical examination of the Malibu Mystique went down as one of SURFER's most innovative—and memorable—articles.

Volume 17 | *Number 2*

CURSE OF THE CHUMASH

BY CARLOS IZAN

1974—A young man, Malibu born and bred, onetime 4A, WSA surf star, son of the chief regional lifeguard, and jack of all trades, crawls out to the point to O.D. for the final time.

1956—Two black Cadillac limousines pull up at the pit on a full-bore hot summer's day in the era prior to total state control. In the limos sit the directors, leading players and author of the screen scenario *Gidget*. They are at Malibu to "soak up atmosphere," scout locations and recruit surfing stand-ins and extras for the film. While the aliens stand on the beach and conspicuously attempt to keep the sand off their wing-tip shoes, several local boys gather bags of human excrement and drop them into the mouths of the limousines' air-conditioning ducts. The cars leave, containing mogul sand stars, travel about 300 yards and stop abruptly while the cast and crew fall out of the cars and gag. Sandra Dee was reportedly observed vomiting on the center lane of the Coast Highway. Tubesteak figures if they hadn't needed air conditioning, it never would have happened.

1964—Two surf groupies from Pacoima set up on the point and promptly administer to the boys' erotic needs. Freddy Hemmings Jr., over from the Islands, sees the melee and is callin' it a good ole Hawaiian train. By 11:30, the passenger count is somewhere around 47. They were still at it 10 hours later, and the caboose was nowhere in sight. Four years later,

Hemmings became world surfing champion, but he is most famous for comparing the Banzai Pipeline to the defensive front four of the Pittsburgh Steelers on national television—ABC's *Wide World of Sports* 1975.

1964—A 90-degree July afternoon: Crazy Kate and a surf star (who shall remain nameless, since he is now married and a well-respected member of the hippie/capitalist business community) had gone into the gray plywood Andy Gump portable sanitation unit to be alone together for their moment of bliss. It being a flat day, the pit crew listlessly followed the grunts and groans of the couple's craven lust. Someone got some baling wire, and the surf rats secured the door latch shut and tipped the outhouse over. The occupants were heard beating on the walls and begging to be saved from their watery grave. The sheriff's rescue squad arrived more than an hour later to pull them out.

1974—The State of the Art: Malibu's being called a clean 7-foot. Bud Browne goes so far as to describe it as the best he's ever seen it. Inside waves are seen throwing out over and completely enclosing the rocks at Old Joe's. Two-hundred-thirty-five miles to the south, the "World Surfing Championships" are held in 3-foot slop at Ocean Beach. The contest was won on a twin-fin.

1854—Andrew Sublett, while walking an old Indian trail in Malibu Canyon, was attacked and mauled by a large grizzly bear. Andrew consid-

ered himself lucky to have gotten away with only a broken arm. Sublett figured that he must have met up with a "friendly grizzly." The California grizzly bear is now extinct.

1962—Lance Carson and the boys are drinking beer out on the point. After his first quart, Lance, without looking, tosses the empty bottle over his shoulder, 22 feet into the barbed wire no-man's land the state has provided to insulate the surfer hordes from the Adamson estate. The house was constructed in 1928 by world-famous architect Stiles-Clements, and movie stars, foreign dignitaries and rich eastern industrialists continually offered millions to buy it. All of this was of no interest to Carson, who proceeds to blindly toss his next two empties onto the same spot as his first. Each succeeding bottle decisively shatters the previous one. It being a hot day, a visitor from the South Bay comments that even if Lance can hit his mark with the now empty fourth quart, there is no way in hell that he will be able to make it to the water. Lance blindly hits the bottle and saunters into the break with his double-ender, where he puts on another of his flawless, polished performances. Climbs, drops, sweeps cutbacks and long-arched nose trims—all of the things that comprised '60s vanguard surfing were second nature to Carson. You see, Lance clearly had the edge 'cause he did it every day.

1947—Dave Sweet and Buzzy Trent are pedaling their balloon-tire junkers up the Coast Highway from the Ocean Park Pier. They have left their boards in the underbrush by the wall at Malibu. They always do this, since the boards are too heavy to carry home on their bicycles. Theft of their surf-boards is out of the question, since they know everyone else who surfs on the coast.

1974—Pacific Palisades. Johnny Fain has ventured into a coin-operated laundromat to use a pay phone. It being strange turf, Fain knows not what to expect, and not expecting anything, he naturally gets the best. A blushing, bleached and powdered, half-curlered, burnt-out cocktail-lounge chippie rushes up. "JOHNNY—JOHNNY FAIN!! Don't you recognize me?" Fain backs off. Uh…I'd probably remember if I…um…had the time, but right now I'm double-parked.

"Johnny!" she screams, "It's me, Gidget. Don't you remember? From Malibu."

Fain remembers all too well. "Um, well I'm still double-parked." Yes, here in the suburban wilderness, Fain has his back up against the 50-cent-a-load commercial drier, and the-honest-to-God original Gidget has his proposed exit path blocked.

Gidget proceeds to tell him all of the details. "I'm married now, got some kids; here's my number; we really ought to get together." Fain shrieks, jumps over the line of Maytags and runs for the door.

"Johnny," she yells after him, "you know married girls like to have fun, too!"

1951—June 15. Perfect Malibu.

1959—August 18. Perfect Malibu.

1976—In the supermarket and department and five-and-dime stores across America, the luscious Malibu Barbie, "a sophisticated teenage doll" with tanned polyvinyl chloride skin, sells for the price of $3.68.

In 1976, photographer Jeff Divine was on hand for the birth of the professional era in Australia. He turned in this nice piece of travelogue capturing Aussie surfing's soulfulness beneath the glitz.

Volume 17 | *Number 3*

ARE YOU HERE TO RAGE OR WHAT?

BY JEFF DIVINE

MICHAEL PETERSON
IN 1976, THE BEST SURFER IN THE WORLD
PHOTO: JEFF DIVINE

Large inch-long red ants scurry across the path as we make our way through the jungle growth and out toward the end of the point. Red and black birds are doing aerial acrobatics between the ghost gum trees and are making loud calls that pierce the quiet beauty as we walk in. The swell can be heard as it crashes against the rocks below us. A cluster of aborigine houses can be seen off in the distance through the trees. The path winds up and down with sharp corners, and finally you come out into a little beach area out on the rocky left point. My first look is through the bushes of an absolutely perfect 6-foot left tube peeling off and spitting as it hits the deep channel area. As I rush out of the bushes and onto the beach, another wave rises out of the deep water, pitches and peels mechanically off the point. I stand on the shell-strewn beach tearing through my backpack for my Nikonos and fins as a third wave pitches over a speed-crouched goofyfoot. It's a very hollow wave, which completely envelops him until it spits him out into the deep channel. Another set approaches as I flop across the sharp, flat, dry reef area with my fins on and Nikonos clutched in my hand. The dry reef area is very similar to the Rocky Point reef in Hawaii. It's very sharp. I swim out to the channel zone right where the wave reaches its hollowest bowl section. There is a lull as I float, slowly kicking and scanning the whole scene. First I stick my head under water and see that the bottom is covered with very big, deep-purple urchins that bristle their spines as the wave currents rush over them. A local surfer paddles by and tells me that an aborigine kid hit bottom recently and had urchin spines stuck all over him, "even in his mouth." Looking toward land, I see more surfers and their ladies, half hidden away, relaxing, soaking rays or shell gathering. High overhead, the clouds are twisting, billowing and patterning into one of those upper-level atmospheric conditions that just adds that much more energy and beauty to the whole place. More waves are approaching as the surfers begin paddling for position, while some of the people on the beach take notice and shift their gaze outside to watch the show. Terry Richardson is coming at me, very carefully shifting rails and setting up for the inside bowl, which pitches out over him as he stands in the shadow smiling and dragging his hand in the face. A chunky older aborigine drops into a very wedgy inside bowl and fires a stylish, powerful backside turn off the bottom and up into the barrel. He paddles back outside, giving me a "G'day, mate" as he goes by. I freak as my leg brushes the bottom; it's only about 4 feet deep where I am floating over the reef, and I think of the masses of urchins just below me. Terry is now fully stoked and proceeds to shred every wave. Air-brushed scenes continuously flash in front of me as Terry comes out of the bowls and throws back into the soup. Every perfect wave has been repeated over and over, continuous sets tube 20 feet from the dry reef front. Donna has now filled a bag full of an assortment of long, curled shells and beautifully colored miniature abalones. As I pull myself out of the water and up onto the reef, Terry's boys are all over me, asking, "Where's Dad?" and as I point outside, the bowl is pitching. Terry has disappeared.

COSMIC SURF
ART: RICK GRIFFIN

The late Bruce Valluzzi, 1960s East Coast star, blazed brightly in the mid-'70s, then burned out like a comet.

Volume 17 | Number 3

WHERE THE LIP DOES NOT LINGER

BY BRUCE VALLUZZI

On an August afternoon, the details of your life demand attention, and you must venture out. All day you have hidden, huddled with the air conditioning, perhaps with drapes drawn, which improves insulation, evading the incessant solar iridescence that impinges itself on the surface of the planet at that point in space. Minimal garb is required gear as you step out the door. The searing, scorching temperature slugs you in the face. Your eyes are bludgeoned by the sunshine. I have stumbled through the human herds of Bombay, when the stench of humanity and cow dung sent me reeling to the filthy Holy Rivers for some relief, and I have grappled with sneak thieves on the fringes of the Sahara when only a well-wielded tire iron sent them fleeing, and those times were only entrées to another summer in the Sunshine State. Perhaps it is the proximity of relief, knowing that in Electrified America, air conditioning cannot be far, while in other lands, one resigns oneself to the fate of slow broil. I do not know. Ocean motion can occasionally arise to provide respite in the form of three-dimensional free verse, but it, even at its best, is by no means the Shakespearean eloquence that recites itself on Polynesian reefs. And in the summer months, the Atlantic is a starstruck fool on some provincial stage who has forgotten every single line.

Woody Woodworth's colorful exposé on the still-untapped Baja surf potential preceded California's late-'70s reassertion of itself as a surf energy center.

Volume 17 | Number 3

IN SEARCH OF THE WARM WIND

A pendulum is put into motion, then two and three, until all the elements are represented.

There before us (the observers of the sea) are the sun, wind and the waves. As the seasonal pendulums swing through time, we notice that those elements will come into sync for brief instants, and hang for times in pairs, but only occasionally come those rare crescendo moments in which we delight, for the pendulums are all swinging together.

Springtime in California, months of change for both the land and sea. To the north, a quiet sets in; the rain and storms have ceased. However, to the deep south, we can visualize a great slumbering giant of turbulent masses of warm air spiraling northwards, sending out thick and well-defined energy bands. Though oftentimes these early rumblings are not as well received, for it is also the time of year when we are unhappy host to the late-night and early-morning low clouds. Daily we are plagued with their presence, the clouds themselves not being

the worst of it. But the onshore winds which accompany them have given this cloud and wind combo the fitting name of the "disasterly duo."

So I say to myself, it's time to hit the road to where the winds are right and the sun is hot.

The cars were loaded, the home fronts secured, and we had two weeks to devote to the task of wave search. Meanwhile, this sleeping giant to the south was due to arise.

It was his energy bands that we were waiting in anticipation of. By this time, however, we were in a land where our giant's efforts would be well received.

. . . There is no camera that can record the ache in your side while laughing around the campfire, or the delight of your first waves after that long and seemingly endless journey. There is also that feeling of fulfillment, your belly full and your body tired as you drift into sleep, knowing that waves will be there in the morning to greet you and your friends, and together you will share.

THE FAMILY AIKAU
"POP," ON THE SECOND ROW, RIGHT
PHOTO: STEVE WILKINGS

A tasty slice of Hawaiiana by former big-wave ace Kimo Hollinger. Eddie Aikau was lost at sea less than one year after this affectionate profile was written.

Volume 17 | *Number 4*

"Pop"

BY KIMO HOLLINGER

As the hour for the luau approached, things got more hectic. Pop was orchestrating to the crescendo. All the ingredients for these far-out Hawaiian dishes had been prepared. All that remained to be done was to mix them together and to add the Hawaiian salt. The amount of salt to be added is very critical. Too much and the dish is spoiled. Too little and the food is tasteless. Pop played this to the hilt. Smiling at his audience, he said, "Hey, Junior, how much you think?" Of course, Junior was noncommittal. "Well," he says, "how about one handful for Hawaii. And one more for Maui. And the last one for Sammy Lee and Kauai." Everyone cheered and got in line to taste. Pop was shouting for Mom to be the first. We all followed. Pop had done it again, perfect. Eddie got all the workers together, and we had a big toast. It was time for me to go home and pick up my family, but how I hated to leave the best show in town.

The luau was a success. Pop was afraid that no one would show up because of the rain that had started to fall, but by the time we got there, it was packed. A parade of musicians came up on stage. The food was delicious. Pop had made enough pineapple swipe to sink (or float) the Lurline. The decorations were outstanding. My daughters could not keep their eyes off the crowd. Holly, who is 12, said, "Daddy, who is that guy over there?" I said, "That's Larry Bertlemann, baby," all the while thinking, "Oh, oh, I'm in for it now." Other notables of the surfing world included Buffalo Keaulana, Conrad Kuhna, Peter Cole, Ricky Grigg and a host of younger cats whose names I don't know. Pop, by this time, was well into his pineapple swipe. One of the dignitaries invited was the Honorable Mayor of the City and County of Honolulu, "Fearless" Frank Fasi. No politician ever wants to play second banana, but what could he do? The last I saw of our mayor, Pop was leading him around by the hand, with the mayor meekly following. At one point, the band was in a full-on boogie, and a cry was heard, "Stop the music!!!" It was Pop. He then mounted the stage, motioning for the noise of the crowd to stop. By this time, everybody was so juiced that God himself couldn't have quieted them. Pop persisted. He finally got the first three rows quiet and made his announcement. I'm trying to remember what it was all about, but I can't, and no difference. It was all just part of the show.

Meanwhile, the rain had really started coming down, and water had collected beneath our feet in great puddles. This in no way deterred the Aikaus. The boys had sheets of plywood in reserve, which they laid down where the people were walking and the worst puddles were. I was apprehensive that my truck was going to sink in the mud and that I'd never get out of there. Reluctantly, I decided to leave. I sought out the members of the family to thank them and to say goodbye. I found Pop in the gaming room. Those dancing eyes by this time were having a hard time focusing, and I wondered how he was managing to maintain. It was about 10:30 then, and I figured he wouldn't see midnight. The professional musicians had since departed, and it was time for Eddie and Clyde to take over. Down home time. I really hated to leave, but the rain, if anything, was coming down harder. I made it to my truck, started her up and eased out the driveway. From the street, I looked down on a scene that except for the automobiles and the electricity could have taken place centuries ago. God bless the Aikaus. Pop made it to three in the morning; the best show in town.

Australian Rabbit Bartholomew announced the new "Free Ride" generation's arrival with authority.

Volume 17 | *Number 5*

BUSTIN' DOWN THE DOOR

BY WAYNE "RABBIT" BARTHOLOMEW

In most articles, we've been given little credit for originality, and many of our peers have expressed criticism toward our whatever. We've been faced with charges ranging from assault and battery to arrogant defiance against the face of waves, and according to some of our peers, the basic flow of our surfing has been lost in a sea of battleground tactics and aggressive abuse of our mother ocean. Apparently, we've also breached the 16th Amendment, in that we've been overampingly gliding with too much glitter. Many minor charges have been submitted, and due to our conquering approach, as Gerry would say, we're experiencing a reign of supremacy within the professional arena, which of course has been thoroughly analyzed and finally diagnosed as probably only a temporary dominance, as we've all supposedly reached our peak. Oh, I shouldn't really get bitchy like that.

TOP: RABBIT BARTHOLOMEW
PHOTOS: ART BREWER

LEFT: RABBIT BARTHOLOMEW
PIPELINE
PHOTO: JEFF DIVINE

John Witzig dispatched the battlefield report from the hotly contested North Shore, fresh in the wake of Rabbit's "Bustin' Down the Door" challenge. The power of a single SURFER feature was never so obvious.

Volume 18 | Number 1

THE NORTH SHORE

BY JOHN WITZIG

LOOKING FORWARD AND LOOKING BACKWARD AND SEEING THE SAME THING

"THERE WAS BARRY AND NAT, AND THEY WERE JUST GOING HEAD-ON. BARRY WOULD TAKE OFF ON A WAVE AND GET BACK INTO IT. AND THEN NAT WOULD TAKE OFF AND GET BACK. PRETTY SOON, BARRY WAS SO FAR GONE YOU COULDN'T SEE HIM...AND THEN NAT WOULD BE IN THE SAME POSITION . . . AFTER THE SURF-OUT, THEY CAME UP ON THE BEACH AND GOT INTO A LITTLE FISTFIGHT. THAT'S HOW THIS THING WAS BOILING OVER." — DAVID NUUHIWA, 1967

When I catch my first sight of Oahu, I can see waves, and I feel like I'm on the edge of a stage. I actually have butterflies in my stomach. I'm a bit scared of what I'm about to get into. Of the reports of threats and violence. Of the big surf. Of knowing that I've always wanted to surf Sunset, and that this is the opportunity. Of simply not knowing if I can do it.

The same applies to the story. I think that I'm lucky in a way. Because partly I'm here just to go surfing. It's a good position to cruise and watch what life on the North Shore is like. But can I even describe what it's like out there trying to ride Sunset? Or trying to gather some of the other threads . . . knowing that I have the opportunity . . . but can I find the story and get it down on paper?

I'm reading the two definitive stories that came out of last winter. Gerry's "Attitude Dancing," and Rabbit's "Bustin' Down the Door." Gerry paints a picture of two opposing styles, the "As," and the "Bs." It seems to me that he's simplified to absurdity. Is he really saying that Shaun's performance is just on a wave; that it lacks an essential relationship to that breaking wave? I watch Shaun, and I find it difficult to believe that anyone could accept that.

And what about the similarities that you can find between Ian and B.K.? Or Mark Warren and Hakman? Sure the patterns are there (and cultural background is a determinant among others), but they are complex and varied things. The analogy with music is too close to ignore. Sometimes there's a base line that you can find common to surfers of divergent temperament and apparent performance . . . but it's there. And it cuts right across any contrived categories as simple as nationality.

Why people are like they are, why surfers surf the way they do, are subjects of the broadest complexity. Just as there are no final answers, so there are no simple ones. . . .

WACK! WACK! WACK!

"OK, I'm the greatest," says Mark Richards, in a parody of "We're Number 1" Ian and Muhammad Bugs. "What sort of year was it?" I ask. "Oh, bloody great, Mate! Well . . . " his voice drops suddenly from the posturing to almost quietly serious, "it was quite different to last year. It was quite radical, because from the start of the winter, there was all that heavy business happening. Luckily enough, I wasn't involved. That was mainly centered around Ian and Rabbit. So the first few days

I was surfing Sunset, there were people paddling up to me and telling me about all the heavy things that were going to happen this year. And I'd say, 'What's going to happen?' and they'd say, 'You'll find out sooner or later.' So for the first few weeks, there were all these people warning me about everything that was happening. And like nothing was happening. Like I was going surfing every day, and the only thing I heard about was Rabbit getting punched out.

"Basically, Aikau cleared it up, because Ian and P.T. and those guys were too paranoid to go surfing. They were staying in the Kuilima watching TV all day . . . and sleeping with tennis racquets . . . and that was true. Like I went up there one night . . . I think it was after they'd been here for a week, and they hadn't been seen, right? And M.W. and I went up . . . knocked on the door, and it was like, 'Who's there? Who's there?' They wouldn't open the door till we identified ourselves. And inside they were just totally paranoid . . . Every time there was a knock on the door or a noise outside, they'd all stop and look around really scared.

"It didn't worry me. Like there was no one after me. I was surfing Sunset every day. It had me a little worried, but I wasn't mentioned as being involved. Luckily enough, I won last year, and I didn't say anything. I said a few things, but they must have overlooked them.

"Then Aikau came around one day and said, 'Look, this thing is getting out of control.'

"Apparently, the meeting was supposed to start at 7, and I got there at a quarter past, and like everybody was sitting in there, and Aikau was sitting up the front . . . he was the head man. There was a seat behind a potted plant in a corner, and I was all ready to beam in on that one, and Eddie says, 'Mark. Up the front, up the front.' So I had to sit up the front. I would've loved to have sat down the back and just watched him up the front and observed everything, but he stuck me right in the middle of it, you know . . . Everyone was watching up front. I guess he just wanted an Australian up the front so it didn't seem totally Hawaiian.

"He said that the main reason for trying to get the thing straightened out was that he didn't want himself or the Hawaiian surfers to win the contests if we weren't surfing our best . . . Like he didn't want us to paddle out scared that if we won we were going to get beaten up as soon as we came in. He wanted us to be totally free to be able to go out and surf as hard as we wanted to surf.

"I think that apparently Hemmings spoke to his father and told him, 'Look. This thing's got to be sorted out.' Hemmings said some really good things at the Smirnoff meeting afterward. He stood up the front, and he said like, 'OK, the Australian guys won last year, and they shot their mouth off, and that's great.' And he stood up there, and he looked at some people; he looked at the Hawaiians, and he glared at them, you know? He said, 'They won; they deserved it. They had the right to say what they felt. No one should take offense to it.'

"But," I said, "They did, didn't they?"

"They did," Mark said, "Yeah. . . ."

"It was pretty serious, and the Hawaiians were worried, too, because some of the Australian articles got produced that said the Hawaiian competitors were beating up the Aussies. And Reno goes, 'We go down there, and what happens to us?' So that was the start of the year.

"The first contest was the Pro Class Trials. Nothing at all happened. There was no anti-Aussie; no one got dudded out unreasonably, and all of a sudden, it was gone. Like you could come here now, and it's just totally unbelievable . . . It sounds outrageous, but it was actually happening. There were actually threats of burning down houses, and of guns and knives . . . and of phantom squads in the night. I can't believe it now.

"I think it's totally changed Rabbit. He's not the same person anymore. Like last year, he was a total aggro in the water. It was nearly impossible to get a wave with him. Now, he doesn't give any away, but he's not like he was. He's much more mellow. I think that it quieted down his approach in the water a little."

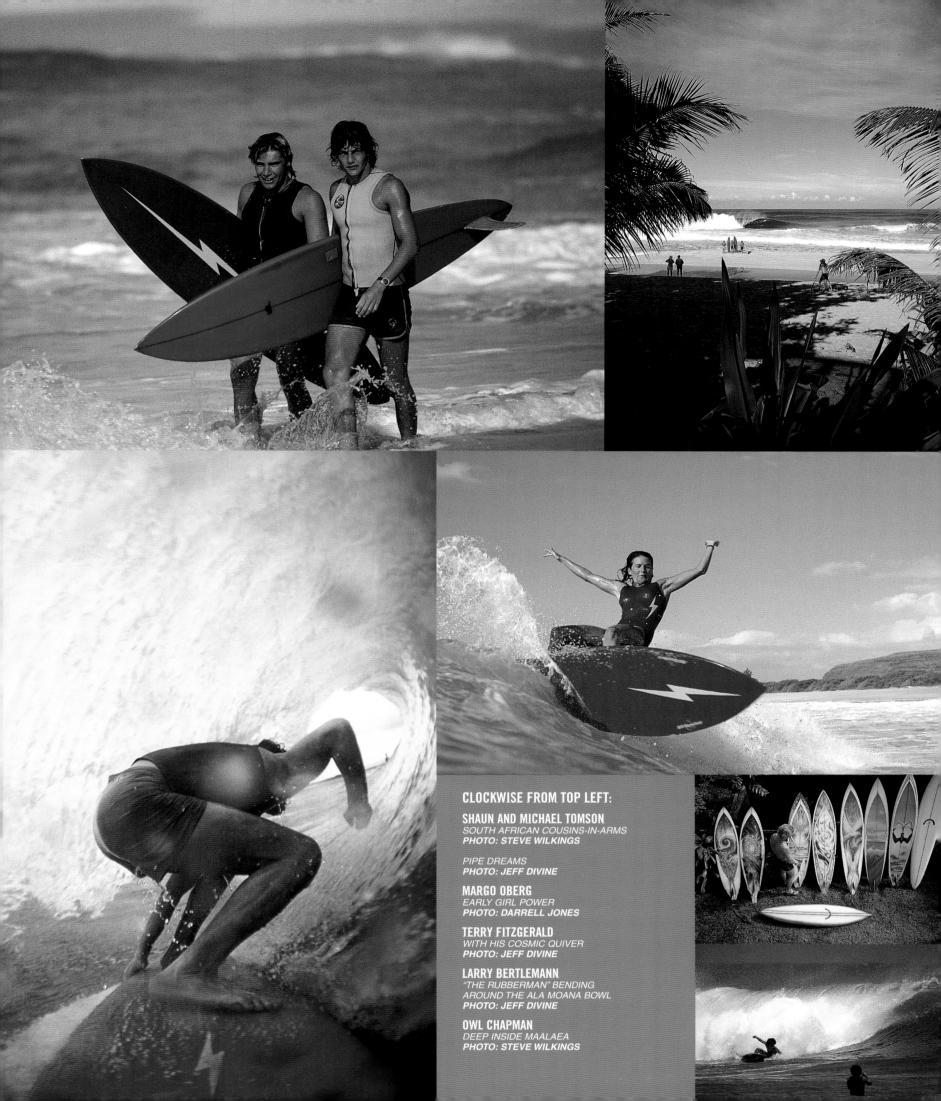

CLOCKWISE FROM TOP LEFT:

SHAUN AND MICHAEL TOMSON
SOUTH AFRICAN COUSINS-IN-ARMS
PHOTO: STEVE WILKINGS

PIPE DREAMS
PHOTO: JEFF DIVINE

MARGO OBERG
EARLY GIRL POWER
PHOTO: DARRELL JONES

TERRY FITZGERALD
WITH HIS COSMIC QUIVER
PHOTO: JEFF DIVINE

LARRY BERTLEMANN
*"THE RUBBERMAN" BENDING
AROUND THE ALA MOANA BOWL*
PHOTO: JEFF DIVINE

OWL CHAPMAN
DEEP INSIDE MAALAEA
PHOTO: STEVE WILKINGS

The always-enigmatic C.R. Stecyk had a unique take on the Hawaiian pro season of 1976–77.

Volume 18 | Number 1

ALOHA-HA

BY C.R. STECYK

It was all too real as I boarded the Honolulu-bound 747 at Hilo International. I had just come over on the mail boat from Kahoolawe and was sweating profusely, since my haphazard travel arrangements had left no room for error. A cursory inspection revealed that the entire jumbo jet was filled with one of those incredible look-alike mainland tour groups. In this case, it was the "Your Man Tour," and the participants were all into their 50s, primed for paradise and flashing those eerie Kodak smiles. The sole distinguishing mark on these individuals was the oval-shaped red, white and blue badge each wore, saying, "Your Man Tours, My Name Is_____."

As I stumbled into the only available seat next to Ruth and Harry Zartler from Sparto, Ill., it was obvious that I wasn't their man. Admittedly, the two-week lack of a shower and shave had ripened me a bit, yet still, the disgusted look on Ruth's face was downright…well…disgusting. I attempted to strike up a conversation to quell the uneasiness: "You folks new to these parts?" etc. Reluctantly, they warmed to my hospitality, and soon I began to discover some fascinating facets of Ruth and Harry's lifestyle. For instance: there was Harry's dry cleaning business that offered the only one-hour Martinizing service in the county; or how Ruth's Oldsmobile 442 could hit 110 flat out and would never start on those cold mornings until Harry mixed cod liver oil in with the Prestone antifreeze; or how Harry figures he walks 50 miles a year shoveling the snow off his driveway; or how the two felt that President Nixon had been framed; and last but not least, how some "teenage hoodlums" stole the "cute" little cast-iron jockey off the lawn in front of their suburban manor (it was a valuable antique, Ruth assured me). Everything was proceeding nicely until Mrs. Zartler sadly stated that their on-flight movie had burned up just prior to the final scene. There the whole flight was waiting for the cinematic conclusion when suddenly the screen filled with the bubbling and crackling visage of burned celluloid. I inquired as to the film's identity and learned it was *The Shootist*, starring John Wayne and Lauren Bacall.

Realizing that this was all that was needed to cement our friendship, I turned to her and said, "Mom, you're in luck 'cause I've seen the film." Her husband was now erect with anticipation. "Well, tell us, how did it end?"

I answered, "Harry. To put it succinctly, John Wayne gets gut shot, and Ronnie Howard avenges his death." Suddenly, old Zartler was beside himself— "You expect me to believe that?" and he shouted, "Hey, here's a laugh, this fellow says John Wayne died at the end, and that the kid who used to be Opie on *The Andy Griffith Show* kills the gunfighters." Total group intimidation . . . rejection . . . alienation . . . all of the "Your Man Tour" was now on my case.

Christ, why did I ever get involved anyway? At least we were landing in Honolulu, and I would never have to see any of their stinking China-white faces again. I knew why they hated me; I had dared to challenge all that they believed in. As I ran down the airport corridor, I could hear Harry chiding me, "Duke Wayne NEVER dies . . . NEVER."

At the customs declaration area, the official hands me a form asking if I have any plants, animals, microorganisms, objects manufactured of vegetal material, firearms, foreign currency, machine tools, etc., to declare. I give him the list back and tell him no. Now I look up and see two crew-cut men in tan leisure suits with 45s bulging under their coats and carrying walkie-talkies across the disembarkation area. It is obvious that they are cops; who else would be wearing coats on an 80-degree day? Having already surpassed my paranoia quota on the journey from Hilo, I figure that there can be no way they're looking for me. However . . . they keep relentlessly advancing, and finally the one with the greasy fenders on his flattop flashes a DEA badge and states: "Mind if we search your baggage?" Meanwhile, Ruth, Harry and the Your Man entourage are watching the roust, wondering if they will ever learn never to trust anyone under 30. While the one DEA agent is feverishly scrutinizing every article of my luggage, the other carries on the inquisition. . . . "Where's your passport?" My less-than-brilliant retort was something to the effect that Kahoolawe was still part of America. Q. . . . "What were you doing on Kahoolawe?" A. . . . "Visiting my grandmother." Numerous Q's and A's follow until the agent of the law grabs me and yells, "Look, boy, nobody ever comes from Kahoolawe; besides, your plane came in through Hilo." The guy's right, and I'm really beginning to wish that I'd never left. Here I am getting the shit hassled out of me in town by these ominous haole DEAs, and all I can think of is how pleasant it used to be living in this very same locale during the territorial days. (Of course, before statehood, any place in Hawaii was a nice place.)

SHAUN TOMSON
TURNING OFF THE WALL TO HIS WILL
PHOTO: STEVE WILKINGS

Now, more pissed than amused, I give the government man a terse lecture on Island history and the spirit of aloha. His cohort, having thoroughly examined everything down to my dirty underpants, is now considering the possibilities for concealment in the 12-foot-long surfboard I'm transporting. He reckons this must be it—it's got to be, nothing else remains—so he holds it up to a wall-mounted fluorescent light fixture, and—FLASH—they can't see anything. "Of course you can't see through it; it's made of Wili Wili wood." I further try to explain that the board is a sacred palo-olo, several hundred years old, and so loaded with mana (accumulated powers) that they had better not mess with it or me anymore 'cause we've both run out of patience. This falls on deaf ears, since even the Drug Enforcement Agency knows that surfboards are all short in length and made from plastic foam (which is precisely why they hold surfboards up to the light to see if there are any telltale contraband shadows inside their volumes).

Now I'm being loaded into this Gestapo looking van, with cops on all four sides of me, and the palo-olo forlornly laying on the floor. This one guy is trying to tell me my rights, and I'm telling him that if I had any rights, I wouldn't be going through all of this.

At airport security headquarters, the boys are Pavlovianly salivating in anticipation of another endless summer hashish surfboard bust. I'm sitting there with the magic surfcraft that undoubtedly belonged to an ancient Hawaiian king, wondering just what sort of kapu these people are going to bring down on us all. Up walks the man with a saw, and I'm screaming, trying to warn them, "don't cut this surfboard; you're messing with powers so heavy that this entire island might be destroyed. You may have taken it too far already." The head guy looks over and says, "Look, son, don't give us any trouble." To which I repled, "I'm not; you guys are in trouble here." Now the leader is calling for some doctors with some psychiatric restraints. Incredibly, I'm being taken involuntarily to a mental hospital, and the retribution these infidels are going to incur is awesome. For, like it or not, the ancient Island gods still reign supreme. A local gentleman in a sweat-stained straw hat comes over and advises them that what I've been saying could well be true. "It's quite possible this is a valuable historical artifact; I suggest you call the Bishop Museum for confirmation," he clearheadedly imparted.

Suddenly, their demeanor changed, perhaps the Kamaaina's advice has swayed them . . . But no, they're drooling again in preparation for another kill. Over at the contraband illuminarium, they are inspecting an Australian's surfboard, and there are these strange opaque cavities deep within its plastic heart. The foreigner informs them that he is a professional surfrider, and that this is a Dick Van Straalen chambered surfboard inserted with Ping-Pong balls for added buoyancy—"It's the compressed air, mate."

Viewing his plight, I know two things for certain: 1. They will shortly dissect his surfboard, and 2. they are doing him a big favor, whether he realizes it or not, because ain't nobody gonna ride big Sunset on a raft of Ping-Pong balls.

The sputtering rose-colored neon light in the airport bar aptly underscored the situation; it kept blinking ALOHA-HA, ALOHA-HA, ALOHA-HA.

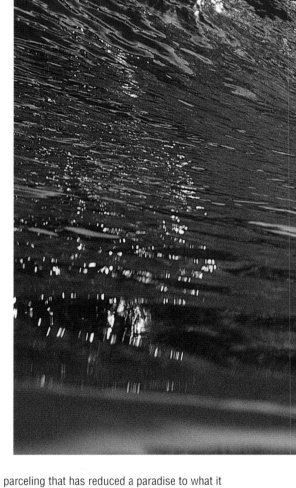

LUNADA BAY
SECRET WINTER HARVEST
PHOTO: WOODY WOODWORTH

RUSSELL SHORT
OXNARD'S FORBIDDEN FRUIT
PHOTO: CRAIG FINEMAN

Even as it rushed to legitimize the growing professional scene, SURFER whispered of values that would ultimately prove more enduring to most of its readers.

Volume 18 | Number 4

THE SECRET THRILL

BY KURT LEDTERMAN

At first, it was so secret only the indigenous Indians knew, but the coastal verities invariably parked themselves in the most cosmic corners and cosmetically clean crannies along the coastline. These Indians are sometimes held in low regard by scholars because of their supposedly slovenly appearance and laziness, but it becomes ever more apparent with time that these Indians were tuned. The Spanish invasion started the land parceling that has reduced a paradise to what it is now. However, even the Indians referred to the L.A. Basin as the Valley of Smokes. And even now, down to today, amid the pollution, population and high Southern California energy, waves may still be found there.

The secret thrill was reborn from Hawaii, carried over by George Freeth, Duke Kahanamoku, and on, rejuiced from the islands by Rabbit Kekai . . . exposed to the California energy and technology by Matt Kivlin, Gard Chapin, Bob Simmons, Tom Blake, Joe Quigg, etc. The thrill was nurtured on the long, smooth, uncrowded waves up and down the coast by a group of misunderstood fools who knew right where they were and were laughing. Their discovery was free utilization of a moving surface, the only wave in a universe of waves, pulses and oscillations that a man could ride. A mesmerizing flow of naturally beautiful energy that could be utilized more functionally by improved surfboard design. An ultimate, functional and aesthetic challenge drawing from the technological advancements possible in a large population of broken-root travelers who were energized all the way to the West Coast. High education, intellectually light industry, plastic cats, centralized and therefore less expensive and more available materials allowed experimenters advances in surfboards impossible in any other area on the planet.

Editor Jim Kempton's easy permissiveness in regard to Hawaiian surfing's drug culture seems almost shocking by today's standards.

Volume 19 | *Number 6*

THE MAGIC OF A HAWAIIAN SUMMER

BY JIM KEMPTON

Night class. Bertlemann's apartment. A case of Miller High Life. Some good pupus. Olomana playing on the stereo. Some dynamite pakalolo. Bertlemann is winding film onto a projector for the night's lecture. The "students" are gathered around. Vince Klyn. Louie Ferrara and his girlfriend. Larry's cousin Wayne. A half-dozen other guys. Larry's lovely wife, Ann, keeps passing mirrors around the room. I am the new pupil trying to find out what is the most magic thing about the summer in Hawaii.

"The magic of Hawaiian summer is when it snows." Larry chuckles at his own comment, and so does everybody else. "No, really, the magic is when the waves come."

"It's more dan magic when dat happens," chimes in Larry's cousin. "It's mo like da kine miracle!" Everybody laughs again.

WAYNE LYNCH
TUNED INTO JOHANNA BEACH
PHOTO: HOULE/McCOY

Now a "mature" surfer at age 25, Wayne Lynch continued to question surfing values, while still leading its performance curve.

Volume 19 | Number 7

WAYNE LYNCH AT 25

BY JOHN WITZIG

Wayne's more cautious than most of the entrapment of position and "eminence." It seems strange in one who seems so young . . . You have to keep reminding yourself that he is 25, and at least as far as you know, he has been expressing much the same view since he was 15. He doesn't want anyone to think that he's smarter than them. Tends not even to think that he is. Doesn't want to be classified in any particular way . . . and certainly nothing in that broad and generally inaccurate group of categories that serve as the homing ground of the idiotic.

He reacts strongly to the idea that he's something of a hypocrite regarding contests . . . that he has a reputation for pouring scorn on them, and that, in fact, he's done very well in them. "No!! I've never said that. The media's saying that. I don't disapprove of them . . . just don't like them. There's a big difference." Given a perfect world, he feels he would say, "No . . . let's have none," but says that he's not trying to identify with a certain anticommercial group. "I have no inclination to do that whatsoever. What I think and how I live is just how I've always done it. I'm not paying out these other guys at all. I think that what they're doing is great if they can handle it. As long as they let me do what I want to do . . . and I'm sure they will."

When *Evolution* hit the surfing screens nearly 10 years ago, its star was just 16. What happened in that early period has strongly marked Wayne's view of the surfing media . . . It's a view characterized by a serious distrust of the star category . . . feeling that often it has little regard for performance. "It goes on regardless, I find . . . because when I had the most publicity, I was surfing probably the lowest I had for two years before . . . and certainly since. That's why I got out and went surfing . . . They put me at the top when I was surfing my worst, and they said I was all over when I wasn't there, and I've had a hundred comebacks according to them. Every time they're ready to think that I'm gone, I like to surprise them. That's my own little game with the whole thing.

"There's a hell of a lot of people just out of the winner's bracket who've got a hell of a lot to give to surfing and who are doing a lot within surfing . . . I don't think that the spotlight falls on them that much." Wayne finds it disappointing that people believe so much of what they read. "It's a pity because I didn't think that surfing would be quite so naive."

He says that he was stunned by the reaction to *Evolution* at the time. "It took me years to really understand what had happened. There was quite a huge reaction to it, you know? I didn't know what to do with it. I just got out of school, and they handed me this and said, 'Here you are, kid, go for it.' What the hell was I going to do with it? I didn't want to be in every magazine. I didn't want to be the f---ing god! If I'd taken that chance, everything would've gone down the chute. I could just see it, and I went 'no.'"

So the virtual retirement was a direct reaction to the youthful stardom? "Of course it was. Direct. But I wasn't 'retired' or wasted or anything . . . All I did was go and live how I'd lived before a few movies. I wanted to get my surfing together, and I knew it wasn't coming together with all those other pressures and all that spotlight attention. So I pissed off to go surfing."

NIAS
PERFECTION IN 1977
PHOTO: ERIK AEDER

Lagundi Bay on Nias, revealed for the first time in this landmark article by Erik Aeder, was the perfect embodiment of the surf traveler's fantasy.

Volume 20 | Number 3

INDONESIA

BY ERIK AEDER

Since nothing lasts forever, the waves had to drop to 2 feet for several days. With the heat, boredom set in, as it was too hot to walk anywhere, too hot to sleep, and I'd been in the ocean for three swims by noon. As our visas were running out soon, but the full moon was approaching, a decision had to be made about leaving. The wounds on my body were pleading with me to stay out of the water for a few days so they could heal up. My stomach longed for good food, and my tongue cried for some ice cream, but I knew that once I was leaving here, I'd be regretting it. I wanted one more chance at the waves, and with the full moon near, we had to stay.

As the moon enlarged, the weather grew dark and the rain came down in torrents segmented by cracks of thunder. The palms were whipped and bent over near the point of breaking, and occasionally a set of coconuts would crash down on the tin roofing. The ocean was stained brown by the flooding river, and the waves were hopelessly unrideable.

That evening, the wind quieted to a purr, and the sky broke clear to reveal the full moon rising behind a curtain of palm trees. After an easy sleep that night, the morning presented us 7-foot swell under overcast skies and a slight drizzle. The rain gave the water surface that texture so you could feel your board through the turns. I stayed out till my arms were jellied, then let a wave wash me over the reef for the last time. We walked back up the beach. I looked over my shoulder through the mist of the shorebreak at another wave on the point that seemed blurringly surrealistic. I rubbed my eyes, then turned and started the short jog through the boonies.

A gentle nudge opened my eyes to a pretty smile and the stewardess saying we were landing soon. I gazed glassy-eyed out the window at the palm-fringed beach passing under us; just another paradise. She asked if I had my customs form ready, and I reached in my pocket to pull out a transparent pink shell, which I handed her. She looked at me, but I was looking out the window again, wondering where I had been.

TIMOTHY LEARY
PHOTO: ART BREWER

Free minds: countercultural icon Timothy Leary's existentialist chat with SURFER editor Steve Pezman.

Volume 20 | Number 8

I'M A BIT LEERY OF TIMOTHY LEARY

BY STEVE PEZMAN

COULD YOU BEGIN BY EXPLAINING YOUR CONCEPT OF THE EVOLUTIONARY SURFER?
Well, we're all attempting to find words and metaphors for processes that are…hard to describe in words. Surfing has always had that problem, as you've already suggested. One of the best ways of describing what we're doing is to define our roles as "evolutionary surfers." Everything is made of waves. At the level of electrons and neutrons, it's part of a wave theory. Historical waves, cultural waves. The more you think about the evolutionary process, the more you see the fundamental structure of nature itself. It's the quantum theory . . . dealing with quantum leaps and quantum waves. Things come packaged in sequential, cyclical, moving, ever-changing forms.

One of the great lessons you learn in the ocean is that while you are totally insignificant to the total mass, you can survive in it by being part of it. Surfing gives you very elemental illustrations of broader truths by serving as a microcosm that we can grasp.

I've been doing a lot of lecturing, and I've picked out as my symbol, surf. I want to have a film of a surfer right at that point moving along constantly right at the edge of the tube. That position is the metaphor of life to me, the highly conscious life. You think of the tube as being the past, and I'm an evolutionary agent, and what I try to do is to be at that point where you're going into the future, but you have to keep in touch with the past . . . There's where you get the power . . . and, sure, you're most helpless, but you also have the most precise control at that moment. And using the past . . . the past is pushing you forward, isn't it? The wave is crashing behind you, yeah? And you can't be slow about it or you [Leary illustrates the lip picking you off]. . . .

But what the evolutionary meaning of it is, you see, I think surfers are truly advanced people. That on any planet like ours, when you get a culture that gets into surfing, it's a sign of maturity on the part of that species. Surfing as we know it now is a very new sport, isn't it?

YES, IT IS.
And although it's almost nontechnological—I mean, it's just a board and the waves—still it can only come from a technological culture in which a lot of power is given to the individual. You see, slaves can't surf or wave slaves can't surf. . . .

The single most influential surfer of the 1970s became so by making it all look easy.

Volume 20 | *Number 8*

GERRY LOPEZ

BY ALLSTON JAMES

Gerry had been out there two hours or more without exactly setting the Pipe on fire, and the gallery in Fat Paul's backyard was getting restless. "He's gettin' old," said Fat Paul, by way of explanation. "Anybody want some more beer?"

A new pack of Heinekens was broken open and half-consumed before the familiar figure appeared, paddling away from the others toward a slightly wider peak. Lopez stood up and drove a straight line through the eye of a monster. Simple and dramatic, and with a touch of class that no one—not the backside brigade, not Russell, Dunn or Crawford, not one of the new wave Pipe aficionados—has yet been able to emulate.

A few minutes later, he was back at Fat Paul's, trading jokes with Flippy Hoffman about the onset of middle age, mingling with the people who knew him before he became an industry. A small, elegant and friendly man who plainly couldn't give a damn that this was the day before the Pipeline Masters, that he'd just had a bad session, and that young hopefuls all along the beach were already spreading the word that Lopez couldn't cut it anymore. At 30, Lopez is used to that sort of speculation. "I was trying like hell out there, but I couldn't catch anything," he joked. "I'm not going to take off on anything where there's a possibility I might not make it. Hey, I'm past that. I can afford to let the 50/50 deals go by. I'm kind of a chicken at heart, and I don't have anything to prove, that's for sure." Later in the month, Lopez the Chickenheart finished in the top six in the Masters, played a starring role for the cameras on the Pipe's best days and headed back to Maui safe in the knowledge that his North Shore performance would keep Lightning Bolt sales figures alive in '79.

Only those who have watched people watching Gerry Lopez surf the Pipeline will understand just what a draw he is. His agility and funky cool in terrifying circumstances are the very essence of surfing's attraction to the masses. Take a kid from Detroit and show him 10 waves of some hot rat tearing up a beach break. Hmm, he'll say, that's clever. Now show him one wave of Lopez blasting out of the horrible bowels of a Pipeline monster in a casual arch. He'll gasp. He'll scream. He'll holler. He'll go mad. He'll go apeshit on surf lust. He'll run from the theater frothing at the mouth, and he'll buy, buy, buy . . . He'll buy three Lightning Bolt surfboards, four T-shirts, two pairs of Bolt board shorts, a neck chain and at least a dozen color posters of the Great God of Pure Source. He'll understand at last what this thing called surfing is all about.

MRS. LOPEZ AND HER SON, GERRY, 1979
PHOTO: BERNIE BAKER

GERRY LOPEZ
LIGHTNING BOLT DROP, PIPELINE
PHOTO: JEFF DIVINE

MARK RICHARDS
*UNFAZED BY PRO SURFING'S GROWING
MASS APPEAL AT THE STUBBIES IN AUSTRALIA*
PHOTO: PETER CRAWFORD

The Australian season wrap-up.

Volume 20 | *Number 9*

WHAT WENT DOWN IN OZ

BY PHIL JARRATT

At approximately 4 p.m. on Friday, April 27, 1979, I managed to extricate myself from a Chinese restaurant in Dixon Street, Sydney, and ran four blocks through the rain to a bar which doubles as an office for some of our city's seedier scribes. I sat myself down, ordered a scotch and soda, reached for the phone and called the lady with whom I share a bed, a pay packet and a variety of complex and somewhat sordid parental responsibilities. "What's happening?" I asked. "You're drunk," she said. "It's Friday," I said, by way of explanation.

"They're flying the Surfabout to Bells Beach first thing in the morning, and they want to know if you want a seat on the plane."

Now, the woman takes gin in the morning and is somewhat given to flights of fancy in the afternoon, but I quickly realized she was incapable of concocting such an elaborate plot as this. I hung up and called my friend Paul Holmes, who for 10 days each year gives up being anyone's friend and becomes the director of the world's richest surfing contest. "What's all this bullshit about going to Bells?" I bellowed down the wire.

"Be at the airport by 6 or we'll give your seat to someone who really cares about the future of professional surfing in this country," he said.

Shaken, I downed my scotch and ordered another. My plans for the weekend had been shot to pieces. Briefly, there were: 1) Drown the hangover with mineral water. 2) Watch Mark Richards win Surfabout '79 in sloppy, 18-inch waves at Narrabeen. 3) Sit down and write the definitive, state of the art piece on Australian surfing for SURFER Magazine, this being the only possible way to salvage something out of the most boring pro surfing season in living memory.

But this was not to be, ah no. Just as things were starting to look up (i.e., the surfers were about to leave town), here was a story. A real live job of work, requiring me to get off my bum, go somewhere and talk to people. The state of the art would have to wait, along with the lawn mowing and car washing. The pro show was off and running. History was in the making. Paul Holmes was going over the wall and he was taking all of us with him.

Chapter Three

The Eighties
Goin' Pro

The Boom Years. SURFER Magazine in the 1980s was like a mighty city trapped in the throes of a gold rush it helped create. Along its once peaceful shores were thrown up the bulwarks of unbridled commerce, as an industry of beachcombers, determined to strike it rich, strip-mined the pure vein of surfing stoke, polluting SURFER's pages with the stink of prosperity.

Or was this just the cynic's cry? Was the self-satisfaction that oozed from each successive issue really smug, or did the growth of the magazine, and the industry it supported, simply represent a new confidence, a more integral sense of authority?

The answers lay between the ads. With the spring-tide swell of the surf fashion industry, suddenly "they" started looking at "our" magazine. Where only a few years previously it had been a forum for philosophy—a doctrine of faith—SURFER morphed into a mainstream marketing vehicle, a window into the world, and the wallets, of a new generation seduced by the surfer's freedom. Represented here, of course, by screen-print T-shirts and bright surf trunks worn without underwear. In the 1980s, it wasn't just that the whole country wanted to dress like surfers, they wanted to dress like the surfers seen in SURFER magazine.

And yet, under all this, there was a conscience. Editor Jim Kempton took the helm at the beginning of the decade, tempering the rush to the mall with a consistent plea for passion. Then Paul Holmes, a displaced Brit who came to the SURFER offices via *Tracks* in Australia, attempted to shepherd an era of international-ism beyond the confines of the professional pro circuit, making SURFER the well at which the global surf village gathered.

Mythology was never completely masked by the marketing. Surfing's world map was expanding beyond imagination—new surf discoveries in Baja California, Costa Rica, Western Australia, Indonesia and the South Pacific kept the dream alive.

There were new heroes, too, and in the bigger, brighter, more pervasive SURFER, their sagas played out monthly. Tom Curren, California's first professional world champion in 1986 and the most dominant personality of the decade, had his ascension inti-mately documented by good friend and SURFER contributing edi-tor Matt George. When he was profiled in a 1987 *Rolling Stone*, complete blocks of copy were lifted straight from a George/SURFER feature.

Curren's antipodal counterpart was Australia's charismatic Mark Occhilupo, but how much of an impact would this young goofyfoot from Sydney have made without the ministrations of Derek Hynd? With his one good eye, the former Top 16 pro and eccentric surf scribe seemed to look deeper into the heart of the '80s pro mentality than was thought possible, to somehow make the concept of being paid to surf compelling to legions of readers who must pay to surf—and pay dearly.

More than anything else, this dichotomy characterized SURFER throughout the 1980s. Much was lost in this period of rapid expansion, as flush with civilian cash-flow, preening under the attention of a voracious society obsessed with youth and wet skin, a certain sluttishness set in; innocence was abandoned, sen-sual integrity compromised. But beneath this—beneath the Day-Glo, Madison Avenue Surf Fetish ads and features about Major League baseball players who liked to surf—SURFER still chal-lenged the same new values it was touting. An article on the resurgence of big wave riding, on the discovery of a new Indonesian dream wave, on Cheyne Horan or any one of the New Centurions—below the gloss was a deeper conviction and always the question: "We do this for love, right?"

CLOCKWISE FROM TOP LEFT:

DANNY KWOCK
NEWPORT POLKA
PHOTO: MIKE MOIR

CHRISTIAN FLETCHER
INTO THE AIR
PHOTO: JEFF DIVINE

SUMMER GLASS
PHOTO: JEFF DIVINE

BIKINI CONTEST BATTLE
PHOTO: JEFF DIVINE

SIMON ANDERSON
THRUSTER INVENTOR
PHOTO: JEFF DIVINE

KEVIN BILLY
EL NIÑO TUBE
PHOTO: JOHN SHETRON

JOHN MILIUS
WAVE-MONGER, WITH TOOLS OF THE TRADE
PHOTO: ART BREWER

Decidedly hawkish screenwriter and director John Milius discussed surfing's role in Francis Ford Coppola's Vietnam epic *Apocalypse Now*, which Milius wrote.

Volume 21 | Number 2

APOCALYPSE NOW

BY JIM KEMPTON AND STEVE PEZMAN

SURFING IS USED AS A MAJOR EXPRESSION OF THE AMERICAN VALUE SYSTEM IN ONE OF THE MOST IMPORTANT SCENES IN THE FILM. COULD YOU TALK ABOUT WHAT HAPPENS IN THAT SCENE AND HOW YOU ENVISIONED IT AS YOU WERE WRITING THE SCRIPT?

Yeah, it's pretty early, about a third of the way, in the big helicopter attack on the Viet Cong village. Kilgore finds out there is a surf spot at the Viet Cong stronghold and decides (against huge odds) to storm the village and take it. And his troops say, "Well, Charlie is pretty thick in there, but there's a good surfing break." So they attack. The idea was that it was supposed to be a left. Kilgore said, "It's a Communist country, you'd think there'd be some left slides!" This is a left point; he's a goofyfoot, and so he really wants to go there.

WHY DID YOU USE SURFING IN A WAR FILM ABOUT VIETNAM?

Vietnam became this clash of cultures, between one culture that was 200 years old and one culture that was thousands of years old. And perhaps the most interesting thing about the culture that was 200 years old is it was manifested most strongly by a subculture that was maybe 10 years old, which was California. And so really what was fascinating about Vietnam was not just that it was an American imposition on Asia, but that it was a California war, and everything about it smacked of that, really. Whereas, if you look at war movies of World War II, you see the guy from Hoboken, and so-and-so is from Flatbush; there's always a guy from Brooklyn, you know. A movie about Vietnam would always have a surfer in it. It was definitely a California war—dope, peace symbols, and rock 'n' roll music more than anything else; fighting to rock 'n' roll music and being stoned, and the kind of outlook of kids who are taken from working on their cars in the San Fernando Valley, and suddenly they're working on helicopters, and they paint "The Acid Queen" on the side of the helicopter and put two extra M-60s on it because this thing is really "Death from Above" [motto of the 333rd Air Cavalry]. And they get into that, and it was a terrific California culture.

PORTRAYING SURFING IN THIS FILM TO THE GENERAL AUDIENCE . . . DO THEY REACT TO IT DIFFERENTLY THAN THE SURFERS IN THE AUDIENCE?

We didn't explain anything about surfing, same as Big Wednesday; I never tried to explain anything about surfing. In the middle of this battle, the aide sees Lance, recognizes him from reading SURFER Magazine, and comes up to Duvall and tells him that Lance is a famous surfer, and then Duvall goes up and shakes his hand. He doesn't introduce himself as Colonel, just, "I'm Bill Kilgore; I'm a goofyfoot." You don't have to tell anyone what a goofyfoot is. Who cares? He goes on to say, "I really enjoy your noseriding and your cutbacks; you have the best cutback in the world." Stuff blowing up all around them and people dying.

WHAT WAS THE IDEA BEHIND KILGORE'S SURF BREAK INVASION? WHERE DID YOU GET THAT FROM?

I put surfing in because it was something I knew and, like I said, the L.A. war, but it really came from an incident in 1967, the Israeli-Arab conflict in which there's an Israeli colonel who led one of the most brilliant armored runs in history, and he was a skin diver. They had pictures of him in *Life* magazine with his goggles on. He brought all of his skin-diving equipment, and he had a very small unit of armor against 10 to 1 odds, broke through all this, chopped up all this Egyptian armor, took his objective, and where his objective was there was a certain kind of fish, abalones or something, that only existed in that area. He had his tanks circled up to the defensive position. He had no gasoline and little ammunition, and he went skin diving, and it was the sort of ultimate kind of counting coup, you know, the slap in the face of the enemy. He was down there; his back was to the sea; he had 10 rounds of ammunition per tank, no gasoline to get out of there, and he says, "I'll go skin diving; I'll take fish from their waters . . . " and I thought that's exactly what a warrior would do. I mean, a warrior would wipe out the place and say, "I will surf their break. I will surf Charlie's point, and I will get tubed, and I will ride well. That's how much disdain I have for the Dinks." And that was the idea of it entirely. Kilgore really caught onto that. He caught onto the idea that it's madness. He takes off his shirt and starts surfing this place, and they're getting fired on from the tree line with mortar fire, and the surfers won't go in, and he says, "You're here; you either surf or fight!" He's crazy but he's not really crazy.

TOM CARROLL
SUNSET STRONGMAN
PHOTO: JEFF DIVINE

TOM CARROLL
JUST A LAD
PHOTO: CRAIG FINEMAN

Bill Barnfield

Veteran Australian surf journalist Phil Jarratt profiled two-time world champ Tom Carroll—along with his inexplicable manager, Peter Mansted—on the comeback trail.

Volume 21 | Number 8

TRUE GRIT

BY PHIL JARRATT

Peter Mansted is frothing at the mouth. Fortunately, it is a telephone conversation and the listener is thus spared physical contact. Mansted is yelling and screaming, and in all probability, jumping up and down on the spot. If he was a wrestling manager on *Rock 'n' Roll Wrestling*, they would go to a commercial, but this is surfing, and the highly controversial manager of the two-time World Surfing Champion will not be shut up. The message is simple, although it is cloaked in the most convoluted claptrap ever to pass for intelligent conversation. The message is that Tom Carroll is coming back! Look out, world, the little

Aussie bleeder is hot to boogie and bust heads! He is gonna make history, says Mansted. He is bigger than anybody; he is the new Martina Navratilova. . . .

He's the what? The new Lendl, Mansted corrects, barely missing a beat. There will be no excuses, no prisoners; the bullshit is finished, washed up, all over. Mansted and Carroll want blood, and they want the title back. And they will get it back!

You put down the phone after a session with Mansted, and you sometimes wonder how much he pays Carroll. And yet there can be no doubt that the huckstering style of the go-for-broke entrepreneur has benefited the surfer, both financially and motivationally. It is a curious—almost bizarre—business relationship that seems to flourish despite the incredible gulf that exists in personal style between the manager and the managed. Mansted is loud and abrasive; Carroll is quiet and, lately, almost spiritual.

A decade or so ago, when he was even smaller than he is now, Tommy used to talk almost exclusively with his eyes. They were manic, super-expressive, bad-ass eyes, and they worked much better than his mouth. In the classic style of the Sydney grommet, Tommy was monosyllabic, almost completely inarticulate. He signaled his intentions—mostly wicked—

by rolling his baby-blues. Out on the water, he was so hot he left vapor trails. On the beach, he was just a funny, freckle-faced kid who often seemed so unsure of himself that the best defense was to pull crazy faces and goon around like a deranged five-year-old. But everyone loved Tommy. He was a funny little bugger—how could you not?

Sitting on the verandah of his home in Newport in early 1987, Tom Carroll waves politely to his girlfriend's mother as she pulls up across the street. "Classic, just classic," he mutters under his breath, enjoying some private joke. Then he lucidly completes the point he was making about asymmetry of surfing and its long-term effect in putting the torso out of sync, before launching into a theory about how mental and athletic conditioning can contrive to defeat purpose, if not kept in proper perspective. Lisa, the beautiful and statuesque girlfriend, squeezes his shoulder as she rushes out to join her mother. "Classic, classic." Tom grins into the middle distance and munches on his bowl of granola. He is 25 years old and he has it all. He has a comfortable house with a rising real estate value, an Alfa Romeo and a beautiful girl, not to mention a dozen thrusters in the spare room. He has it all, except the world title he lost a year ago. And now he wants it back.

More than 10 years after "We're Tops Now," John Witzig returned to California and produced a critical three-part series about West Coast surfing—with the exception of this one cheerful segment.

Volume 22 | *Number 1*

The Tropic of Cancer?

BY JOHN WITZIG

IT'S BEEN VERY NICE TO KNOW ME

This is just another California story. Despite what the editors will try to tell you, it isn't the definitive article on surfing in that diverse state. They couldn't find a local who was stupid enough to generalize to the degree desired. . . . Up shot my hand. . . . "Me, sir! Me! I'll say anything." Well, I spent the better part of a month wandering

swell.) Always an idiot, I agreed. That was a bit before midnight.

By about 1 a.m., there was a small expeditionary force of Sam and Matt George, Tommy Curren and two Australians assembled. Sam and Matt are actually quite different people. One talks more, and one laughs louder. But somehow, it's difficult to think of them as

clothes, and packs to stuff them in. The enthusiasm was undiminished. When we got to Gaviota in Old Yeller, there was no swell. Still, we told each other, remember that time when it looked flat and whatsitsname was 4 feet at dawn? We were undeterred even by a crew who'd been in by boat and said it was quite flat. They, we figured, were proba-

TOM CURREN
AT FIFTEEN: INCUBATING HIS DESTINY AT RINCON
PHOTO: CRAIG FINEMAN

around the coast. It was pretty much fun, and it was at the magazine's expense.

2002s, 320Is AND 530s

The reporter wanted to see the Ranch again, but there was some difficulty. None of the rich trendies would let me in, I was complaining to a bloke I met at a party in Montecito. Why don't we walk in, he said? I have this sneaking suspicion that the questioner wasn't looking for an affirmative answer. (There was no sign of

other than a complementary pair. Both bubble with an enthusiasm that is happily contagious, and both are good surfers.

Tommy Curren is a hot surfer. He's 14 or 15 (I forgot to ask), and while I hate to put a jinx on him, if anyone I saw in California is likely to do a Rolf Aurness, then I'd imagine it'd be Tommy. Whether he wants to or not—even he's not sure yet. He seems to suppose so. He tells some funny dirty stories.

By 1 a.m., we had borrowed food and

bly Valleys who wouldn't recognize a wave if they fell over it.

And so we walked in. Not after some agonizing about the right way that this should be accomplished. The beach-and-rocks route was ruled out by purely practical considerations. It was high tide and you'd have had a difficult enough time trying had it been broad daylight. On a dark night it was ridiculous. Besides, we like the idea of staying dry. We might, we thought, have to cut down by the cliffs to get past the guard post, but reckoned that the railway line provided the straightest, driest and altogether quite the simplest way in.

We thought that we were pretty clever as we sneaked past the guard by keeping in the shadow of the inland cutting. We did it one by one. Good war games. Exciting even. On the way back, we just wandered through as a group. No one took the faintest notice.

By 2 a.m., we were approaching Razorblades where we agreed we'd decide if it's worth going any farther. It really was flat. It was barely bothering to break. So we sat down at the northern end of that trestle bridge, and we had an early breakfast of bananas and some disgusting cake that tasted terrific, and we passed the water bottle around. The spirit of camaraderie that had accompanied us thus far didn't desert now.

Sam or Matt had an idea. There would almost certainly be waves at Jalama. If we walked back (there really being no reason at all to go on), we could drive to Jalama and be there about dawn. And since going back to Santa Barbara without having gotten in the water would be an admission of defeat of the worst kind, it was agreed.

If the meal at Razorblades had been memorable, then the landscape near Jalama, predawn, was equally so. It is a most beautiful bit of country. I think it was perhaps the first time that I've seen forests of those black-green oaks that remind me so much of Spain. There had been a lot of rain, but in the early summer, the hills were already browning. The contrast between it and the trees is at once subtle and spectacular.

There were waves at Jalama. It was also bloody cold. I wanted to wait at least till the sun had cleared the hills behind us. Nothing would deter the enthusiastic Sam. He said that 56 degrees was warm. I didn't, of course, accept the argument until he came in, and I used it to convince him that he didn't need his booties. Matt said that it was our "duty." Everyone hit the water eventually, quick, with an excellent wave sense. Sam was next. I brought up a long last. But in the spirit of the occasion, Sam and Matt might just about have granted me "waterman" status for the day (had they thought about it).

FROM LEFT: AL MERRICK, DAVEY SMITH AND MATT GEORGE
STROLLING PAST THE PAST AT THE 'CON
PHOTO: JAMES METYKO

Mark Richards, four-time world champion from Australia, dominated pro surfing in the early '80s despite his "surfer next door" demeanor.

Volume 21 | Number 8

MR. HUMBLE

BY PHIL JARRATT

The conversation had turned full cycle. Humble had won the day. M.R. really is humble despite the bravado. He's the world champion but he can't do laybacks. He tells this story: "The first time I saw anyone do a layback wasn't Dane or one of those guys. It was a little kid down at Chuns. I watched this little kid do it, just lie down and get up again, and I paddled over to him and asked him how he did it. The kid just laughed at me, thought I was joking. I said, listen, I'm serious. I want you to teach me. He said, oh, it's easy, you just lie down in the water and get up again. Can you believe that? You just lie down and get up again! God, I was in shock."

M.R. turned 23 on the first day of the Stubbies. He's quite a wealthy young man. Forty grand plus last year, that kind of wealthy. And he's still stoked. He says he hates contests but he plans to go on winning them. I hope he does, because I love to watch him glide . . . take off and swoop and glide. It's the sort of surfing that brings out the worst clichés in surf writers and the best responses from jaded judges who've seen it all. I hope he goes on winning, because he's done as much for the art as the sport, and he's just a big, gangly goof that you can't help but like . . . Everybody likes M.R.

M.R., O.P., H.B.
PHOTO: JEFF DIVINE

THIS PAGE: MR. HUMBLE
PHOTO: NORMAN SEEFF

RIGHT: MARK RICHARDS
AT THE BILLABONG PRO, WAIMEA BAY
PHOTO: WARREN BOLSTER

MOROCCAN SURF HAREM
PHOTO: ART BREWER

Team Lightning Bolt, led by Rory Russell, Art Brewer and surf journo Bruce Valluzzi, debauched themselves through 1,001 Moorish nights.

Volume 23 | Number 9

BY BRUCE VALUZZI

A sarcastic wind ruffled the bay and rude noises annoyed the dawn as traffic jostled aboard the boat in Algeciras. Our tickets said "Africa Flash." How true. The passengers were a collection of seedy men in rumpled suits, hooded Arabs, German skinheads, some overripe goat farmers (the fragrance told the tale), truck drivers, assorted creeps, weirdos and, of course, us. Standard fare on the boat to Morocco. *Maroc* is French for *Morocco*, and "us" was Team Maroc: Art Brewer, Rory Russell and I. Brewer, you may remember, is the largest and fearless "Don" of surf photography, easily given to thundering tantrums, who thinks Helmut Newton is a pussy-whipped choirboy. Russell is the Pipeline Tubemaster whose game is audio/visual entertainment for the Bolt Corporation but who, once out of Big Duke's sight, clutching an expense check, becomes a demented Pleasure Hound hell-bent on sniffing out every willing wench and sleazy beer joint from Laguna Beach to Marrakesh.

In Lisbon five days earlier, these two stumbled off the plane from New York at 7 a.m., swilling the dregs of a quart of Jack Daniel's. Rory tried to hustle the stewardesses while he flashed the grin of a convicted sex offender . . . I sensed trouble. The plan was to drive to Morocco, shoot an article for SURFER Magazine, then hook up with a film crew from ABC's *American Sportsman*. They had just won an Emmy for their piece on surfing in Indonesia and were ready for a sequel. Our trip was a modular enterprise organized independently of them that plugged neatly into their "exotic locale" format. Management hoped the dual tasks would squelch the ludicrous tendencies inherent in a trio of notorious screw-ups. After hanging around Portugal a few days, hoping the 15-foot storm surf would clean up (it didn't), it was obvious their worst fears were justified. This was to be another episode out there with the lunatic fringe. We trespassed all boundaries of social outrage, lechery, drunkenness and bad breath. In short, we were on a surf trip.

I was relieved to be on the boat, off the Iberian Peninsula. Surely it was just a matter of time before the Guardia Civil closed in for the kill, leading a horde of irate villagers waving axes who remembered us from "The Sweet Garden of Maria," a roadhouse in our recent past. A covey of truck drivers was drinking quietly when we blundered in the place sometime after midnight, fired up the jukebox and demanded beer and espresso. The commotion awoke Maria, the barman's daughter, who wandered out of the back room in her nightshirt, a real cutie. It was lust at first sight, and Brewer sprang into action. He focused his fish eye in on her young cleavage, and while his motor-drive was blasting away assured everybody in the place it was perfectly proper. He was, he explained, on personal assignment from King Juan Carlos, a geologic survey, you understand, and this was some terrain The King just had to see. The jukebox was blaring Rod Stewart's "Passion" ("everybody needs some"), but the Spanish truckers weren't going for it. The mood turned mean, and an ugly crowd formed around Brewer. Things looked grim, so I lobbed a flaming roll of toilet paper into their midst, grabbed a CO_2 extinguisher off the wall and gassed the mob, screaming, "FIRE! FIRE! RUN FOR YOUR LIVES!" Blinded by the fumes, the truckers crushed each others' toes as they tried to stomp the flames out with their hobnail boots and fistfights erupted. Everybody was yelling, then furniture started flying. Team Maroc slipped out in the clouds and coughing and confusion.

We were on the boat but wouldn't be safe until the line was cast off. If they caught us, we could expect special vengeance from the parents of the shepherd girl who had stumbled on me guzzling a beer and peeing simultaneously. She was traumatized, her sense of digestion distorted forever.

PIPELINE
TAKES A BITE
PHOTO: TOM SERVAIS

TOAD stood for "Take Off and Die." Enough said.

Volume 24 | Number 3

TOADS

BY NEIL STEBBINS

I AM A TOAD. Mind you, I wasn't always one, but after blasting a few thousand beginners at beachbreaks, I graduated to pounding weekend crowds at Malibu. Two years at the 'Bu and a summer in Hawaii gave me a taste for struggling bodies, and since then, I have become rather piggy when it comes to helpless paddlers caught inside. But I digress. I should tell you about a TOAD's life and a TOAD's world, our preferences and tricks of the

trade. First of all, TOADs travel a lot to eat. I've tasted Ops at the Wedge, snacked on Quiksilvers at Bondi, eaten the occasional bikini in South Africa and got very chubby a few winters back on the North Shore. (I love the taste of fried Hawaiians, but I usually have to settle for haole burgers.) Some of my friends (a TOAD's friend is usually another TOAD) travel out of the tropics quite a bit, but I personally don't care for neoprene. Too chewy. Board cords do make good dental floss, though, and they are more common in colder water. Nevertheless, I do all right. I ate a tandem team yesterday at San Onofre, and there's a contest in San Diego this weekend, so I should be able to grub up a few gremmies on my way south. Contest surfers are not usually very appetizing—in fact, a lot of them are just plain tough—but if there's a WISA heat or two, I should be able to select a few tasty morsels out of the herd. I love it when they squirm on the way down.

Traveling takes energy, of course, so a TOAD's life is devoted to food. I've been known to swallow absentminded low-flying pelicans, but birds and the occasional Jet Skier are just junk food for any true TOAD. Wave riders are by far the most challenging and satisfying sort of sustenance. People ask me what surf stars I've eaten and who my favorites are, but it's hard to say. Bronzed Aussies are good, and I am very fond of Rabbit, but Michael Ho and young Mark Foo (Mark Foo Yung?) always leave me hungry an hour later. I ate a photographer once—Divine—and I do like Buffalo once in a while. Shaun the Prawn was digestible, and I suppose Rory was all right—if you like dog—but, when it comes to mainland delicacies, it's Tubesteaks for this TOAD. Anyway, it's getting time for me to eat again, although it's been nice talking to you. Perhaps we can meet for a bite sometime. You just name the time and place, and bring your favorite surfboard. The lunch will be on me.

Volume 24 | Number 5

CALIFORNIA STORM SURF

"On one spectacular triple-overhead wave, resembling Outer Reef Pipeline, Chris Barela dropped-in, cranked a tight bottom turn, disappeared into the huge tube, then got spit out in hands-up position. The cheering and hooting from the beach crowd was deafening. There was not any contest rating, prize money or trophies, but every surfer in the water was a hero in this pounding storm surf." — STEVE SAKAMOTO

CLOCKWISE FROM TOP LEFT:

CHRIS BARELA
BIG REDONDO BREAKWALL
PHOTO: STEVE SAKAMOTO

JOEY BURAN
SEEKING THE LIGHT AT OCEANSIDE
PHOTO: SONNY MILLER

NEWPORT
PHOTO: MIKE MOIR

JOHN MCCLURE
HIGH-QUALITY CALIFORNIA
PHOTO: CRAIG FINEMAN

RUSSELL SHORT
VENTURA CLASS
PHOTO: CRAIG FINEMAN

The formerly glamorous world of big-wave riding was so eclipsed by the burgeoning pro circuit that by 1982 this provocative question required asking.

Volume 24 | *Number 5*

WHATEVER HAPPENED TO BIG-WAVE RIDING?

BY LEONARD BRADY

Twelve lets you enter the game. Twenty makes you a player. Twenty-five, thirty, and hardly anyone wants to play anymore. Thirty-five—James Jones, Clyde, Bradshaw and maybe just a handful more in the entire surfing world have it in their hearts not only to be out in that deep blue lineup, but to be scrambling for the baddest of the biggest set waves. What happened? Have surfers turned into candyasses? Is surfing now a viable alternative to general wimpdom?

MIKE PARSONS
ISLA TODOS SANTOS, CIRCA 1989
PHOTO: TOM SERVAIS

JAMES JONES
ON THE LAST EMPTY DAY AT WAIMEA
PHOTO: BRIAN BIELMANN

JACKY GRAYSON
*GUERRILLA-SURFING
WAR-TORN EL SALVADOR*
PHOTO: DARRELL JONES

Sponsored surf trips began to take on a mercenary flair—with or without a civil war to contend with.

Volume 24 | Number 10

COMBAT SURF

BY RAFAEL LIMA

On the rocky point that juts out in the Pacific rests Punta Roca Restaurante, a small cinder-block building amidst a stand of trees, with a tiled porch littered with rickety wooden chairs and tables. Perched on a stone wall, his back to the water, an Indio strums an ancient guitar. On the porch at Punta Roca Restaurante, not much has changed; the war has left La Libertad relatively quiet. A drunk Indio in a beat-up straw hat sways unsteadily past the restaurant, walking barefoot along a dirt road.

The last time I was here, I spent the afternoon in the capital, San Salvador, after a university demonstration had turned bad, watching the steps of a cathedral literally swarming with people, crawling with people, one lying atop the other, writhing like worms, trying desperately to escape the well-placed, devastating small-arms fire from the Salvadorean military. I was lying face-down on the hot pavement, watching the fierce automatic weapons fire spatter concrete all around the cathedral, rounds ripping through the sheet metal of the parked cars near me, shattering windows and raining glass, the deafening sound of assault rifles everywhere, watching one peasant man in a baggy cotton shirt and a straw hat trying to drag another man toward cover, dropping him after an automatic burst shattered a car window near him, grab the wounded man again and step toward a doorway only to stumble and fall as a line of spattering concrete cut a line across his legs, his pants suddenly splashed with blood.

That had been two years ago, and now the fighting had moved to the countryside. San Salvador, like La Libertad, was relatively quiet, and I was back to go surfing. On that expedition, I'd also been with Darrell Jones, a friend whom I had first met 14 years ago on a cold winter ground-swell day at South Beach. He had become a soul mate and traveling companion. Darrell and I had made our way from the capital city of Guatemala to a tiny town on the Atlantic coast near the Honduran border called Chicimula. I had been hired by an American company to train militia men in anti-insurgency and light weapons. Darrell had come along as a photographer and because "it sounded like fun" and we might even catch some waves.

EL SALVADOR
LA LIBERTAD BEACH PATROL
PHOTO: DARRELL JONES

GERRY LOPEZ
WITH A POETIC APPROACH TO GNARLY G-LAND
PHOTO: ERIK AEDER

Surfing's ultimate stylist Gerry Lopez amazed readers as much with his meticulous calligraphy as with his surfing at the Grajagan surf camp.

Volume 25 | Number 2

JAVA DIARY

BY GERRY LOPEZ

6/25 SURFED THE LOW TIDE OUTER COVE LAST EVENING & ENJOYED NOT ONLY SOME OF THE FINEST FUNNEST HOT DOG WAVES WE'VE HAD BUT ALSO A GREAT SUNSET FROM THE WATER - THE WHOLE CHARACTER OF THE OCEAN CHANGES ONCE THE SUN GOES DOWN BUT IT IS THE SMELL THAT IS MOST NOTICEABLY DIFFERENT. STRONG & PUNGENT, LIKE SOMETHING YOU MIGHT ASSOCIATE WITH THE LOST SHIPS OF THE SARGASSO SEA - KINDA SPOOKY. BUT THE WAVES BEFORE THAT WERE SOMETHING - JUST YOSHI, JAKE, MONGO & MORE WAVES THAN WE COULD HANDLE - SOME STAND UP SET-UPS, EASY-IN, EASY-OUT & DRY THE WHOLE WAY. THAT'S ACTUALLY THE ONLY TIME I'VE EVER SEEN IT TUBE UP IN THE COVE - DEFINITELY ONE OF THE MORE MEMORABLE EVENING GO-OUTS. AN AMERICAN COUPLE SHOWED UP YESTERDAY, APPARENTLY UNATTACHED, BUT HOLDING VALID JUNGLE PERMITS. THEY HAD ORGANIZED THEIR OWN SUPPLIES & TRANSPORT WITHOUT ANY LOCAL ASSISTANCE & CAUGHT A RIDE INTO CAMP ON OUR SUPPLY BOAT. THEIR SPIRIT OF ADVENTURE IS ADMIRABLE BUT I DON'T BELIEVE ANY DEGREE OF COMFORT EXISTS IN THIS APPROACH AS THEY PLAN TO STAY TWO WEEKS BUT HAVE FOOD & WATER FOR LESS THAN HALF THAT LONG. BEING HUNGRY & DIRTY DOESN'T SEEM LIKE MUCH FUN. (CANNON FODDER - A ROMAN MILITARY WRITER ONCE SAID, " THAT NO GREAT DEPENDENCE SHOULD BE PLACED ON THE EAGERNESS OF YOUNG MEN IN COMBAT, FOR THE PROSPECT OF FIGHTING IS AGREEABLE TO THOSE WHO ARE STRANGERS TO IT.") WE SHALL STAND BACK & LET THE JUNGLE DO ITS WORK. THE TIDE TODAY IS A 22/1000 HRS. , ENOUGH WATER TO EFFECTIVELY SQUELCH THE LITTLE SWELL - THE TIDE SEEMS TO COME IN A LOT SLOWER THAN IT GOES OUT. BIG MIKE, J.P. & PETEY FLYING IN ON THE LITTLE RADON SHUTTLE SERVICE - EXTRAVAGANT BUT ALSO NICE & QUICK AS COMPARED TO OVERLAND HOWEVER YOU BETTER BE SURE YOUR SHIT'S TOGETHER - NO COAST GUARD TO CALL FOR HELP. TODAY WE SURFED THE BACKSIDE OF THE HIGH TIDE, LOOKING FOR THAT FALLING TIDE PUSH & FINALLY TIMED IT RIGHT. THERE IS MASSIVE EVIDENCE POINTING TO THE FACT THAT MAYBE G-LAND IS A LOW TIDE BREAK. WENT OUT FOR THE EVENING SHOT AS WELL, INCONSISTANT BUT CLEAN - THIS SWELL EBBING DOWN MUCH FASTER THAN THE ONE BEFORE. WELL THE NEW GANG COMETH & THE OLD GANG GOETH & ALWAYS A LITTLE SADLY AS WE HAVE GROWN A LOT CLOSER TOGETHER BEING SO ISOLATED OUT HERE IN THE JUNGLE. WE HAVE LEARNED A LOT FROM THE YOUNGSTERS, PLAINLY THEIR RANGE IS MUCH BROADER BECAUSE THEIR ROOTS ARE IN JUNK WAVES & GOOD SURFBOARDS. WHEN WE BEGAN, WE HAD GOOD WAVES, LESS PEOPLE IN THE WATER & FLINTSTONE EQUIPMENT BUT THEN WE WERE ONLY OUT TO RIDE THE EASY PERFECT WAVES WHILE THESE KIDS BEGAN THEIR CAREERS ON HIGHLY TUNED BOARDS IN SLOP SURF. GOING FAST ON A GOOD BIG WAVE IS SIMPLE BUT GOING FASTER ON SMALL JUNK SURF IS WHAT THE NEW WAVE IS ALL ABOUT. OLD AGE & TREACHERY NEVER HAD A CHANCE AGAINST YOUTH & ENTHUSIASM EVER.

While attending photography school in Santa Barbara, Texas-born Jim Metyko was on hand to document a very influential stage of West Coast surfing development— and make some very influential friends.

Volume 25 | *Number 5*

GOOD-BYE, CALIFORNIA

BY JIM METYKO

TOM CURREN

There has only been one major change in Tom's life since I met him. A good one at that. He married a beautiful girl named Marie. Allow room in a car for two people, two wetsuits, Tom's thruster and Marie's "truster" (thruster with cute French accent). Everything else? The same. Now he is one of the best surfers in the world. But everybody knew he would be. No, he just hasn't changed.

Still, even today, no song is played in its entirety on the radio before the dial is turned. Except the Who.

"Can I have a piece of gum?" means nearly the whole precious pack.

"Your car or my car?" always means your car.

"Are you getting something to drink?" means get him something, too.

And, best of all, he still gives that hole-in-the-pockets look when you ask for gas money.

It is that lack of change that is the best thing about Tom. He has the surfer's dream, and for better or worse, he doesn't let it interfere with him being him and just going surfing.

LEFT: TOM CURREN
COMING INTO HIS OWN CUTBACK
PHOTO: JIM METYKO

DAVEY SMITH
IMPATIENT DAWN PATROL
PHOTO: JIM METYKO

DAVEY SMITH

He is one of the few surfers who wants to get up earlier than me. "Let's leave at 6:00," I'll suggest. No, he'll say, 5:00. Before the conversation is over he'll have me picking him up at 4:30. I'll get there 15 minutes early to show him I can handle it. And he will be waiting on the curb—impatiently.

For Davey, the sooner he leaves, the sooner he will get to his 50-mile drive, 30-minute walk, oversize northern reef break. And it's worth the loss of sleep, the drive, the walk and rugged conditions to see and photograph him there. This is where the real Davey Smith surfing takes place. Don't count on it at a surf contest in Huntington. Here his surfing is spontaneous and innovative to the point where you never know what he will do next, and sometimes you don't even quite know what he did last.

If Tommy is one of a handful who does today's surfing at its best, Davey is one of those even more rare types who constantly redefines it.

So you get out of the water at 12:00 and make the 30-minute walk back and snack at the only burger spot for 50 miles, sit a little bit and then it's time for a decision—another surf or go home. As it is, you wouldn't get home 'til 2:00 and the surf is blowing out. But you're with Davey. There never really was a decision to make. You grab your stuff, psych up and start walking.

It's dark now. You're dropping Davey off. "Let's hit it tomorrow morning at 6:00," you suggest. He says, "5:00." This time you show up at 4:00. On his door is a message: "Jimmy—Couldn't wait. See ya there."

DAVEY SMITH
EARLY AERIAL SEQUENCE
PHOTOS: JIM METYKO

KEVIN NAUGHTON
*THE STUFF DREAMS AND VISA-CARD
VACATIONS ARE MADE OF, TAVARUA*
PHOTO: CRAIG PETERSON

SURFER reinvents the dream with the world's first look at Fiji's Tavarua island surf resort. Who better than '70s travel icons Craig Peterson and Kevin Naughton to tell the tale?

Volume 25 | Number 12

TAVARUA

BY KEVIN NAUGHTON

"Try opening your eyes," advised Craig as I paddled by.

"What?" My jaded senses hadn't quite recovered from the last coral-crushing wipeout. Water and reef were still pouring out of my ears.

"Yeah. Try keeping your eyes open under water," he added from the channel where he bobbed safely on an air mattress. "It's so clear and swirling, just like fast-motion clouds! It'll take your mind off the next wipeout."

Was he serious? Telling me how to enjoy the beating of my life in 8- to 10-foot surf detonating over a shallow and sharp coral reef? Surfing along the lines of responsibilities in California over the past few years had not prepared me for these steep and fast Fijian waves. Possibly the best waves we'd seen on any of our travels. The pummeling I was getting couldn't quench the special thrill of surfing open-ocean waves in the South Pacific. But suggestions from Peterson's gallery in the channel were more than I could bear.

While paddling back outside, I wondered how we came to experience this gut-rush excitement of surf exploration in Fiji.

Only a few weeks earlier, Craig and I were bracing ourselves for the summer onslaught of tourists flooding Southern California's suburban wasteland. At one time, Peterson's talent was making flight reservations to exotic locales. Nowadays, his efforts focused on making reservations for two, with bikini-clad talent, at a local watering hole charging airfare prices for exotic drinks.

Throughout the '70s Craig and I could probably be found only by a search party. We forged our way through the jungles and deserts of Africa, Central America, Mexico and South America, lived like Gypsies in Europe, and hopped cargo flights and mail boats to esoteric islands. What we usually discovered were the places not to go for good surf. In the '80s it's our creditors who are organizing the search parties ("I always pay by 'traveler checks': next time you're traveling through, check with me!").

We'd long ago shelved all travel exploration plans. Imagine our dilemma when career commitments conflicted with an offer from two friends to surf classic waves on a private South Pacific island. Was there any real choice in the matter?

Following frenzied preparation, it was only a matter of weeks before we had burned our career bridges (yet again) to take Dave Clark and Scott Funk up on their offer. It wasn't difficult finding a media and windsurf crew (hundreds of applicants, mostly female, were screened in just a few days). The lucky recipients of the three remaining invitations were filmmaker Greg Huglin and windsurfers extraordinaire Rich Myers and Suzanne Gedayloo.

Now here we were in a separate reality. We had arrived. Four miles away sat the closest bit of land: a lush, tiny tropical island on which we had earlier enjoyed breakfast served by a lovely lady. And far beyond that island rose the sugar-caned hills of the main island, where a hundred years ago we could have been the catch of the day for roving cannibals in their war canoes. Timing is everything.

And I knew my timing was off this day as, on my very next wave, wide-eyed under water, I saw how humiliating it must be to fall into a giant washing machine and drown in the warm suds cycle.

"Hey! I've got all the wipeout shots I need. Now try making a few," shouted Peterson.

I'd heard enough of his condescending advice. It was time for the perfect surfing crime. Revenge would be sweet on this open-ocean reef, far from any witnesses, save for the boat anchored nearby, tugging like a horse reined to a hitching post in the channel swells.

Yes, time for Peterson to get some "real" close-ups. That would be my angle to lure him deep into the lineup. From all game fishing in Fijian waters, I liked the idea of hooking that yellow-finned photographer onto the coral reef with his eyes wide open. Flailing my arms like a rod with a 50-pound tuna on the end, I directed him toward a set staircasing on the horizon. The huge set swung wide while he unsuspectingly flapped his way into the impact zone, right near the reef boil that had been causing my knees to chatter like a pair of cheap maracas all day.

Edging over the feathering crest of the first wave, already past vertical, I caught a glimpse of what seemed like an infinite number of swells stretching to the horizon. I looked back to see a confused Peterson thrashing and cursing madly, and with a feeling of glee, I saw he had taken the bait. Between the thunder of waves, I knew from his screams that it wasn't a shark attack. No shark could survive that impact.

Even so, I could expect not only survival from Peterson, but worse still, retaliation.

**CRAIG PETERSON (LEFT)
AND KEVIN NAUGHTON (RIGHT)**
PHOTO: TOM SERVAIS

What happened to big-wave riding? This single incident, as Hawaiian surfers James Jones, Mark Foo, Alec Cooke and J.P. Patterson faced "the biggest wave ever dealt with by man."

Volume 26 | Number 7

WILD WAIMEA

BY JAMES JONES

Suddenly I saw it coming, the biggest, most enormous wave I'd ever seen from the water. From the moment I saw it coming over the horizon, I knew we'd never make it. I scratched the water frantically, paddling out to sea with the other three far behind me. The wave walled up all the way across the bay and peaked, not at either side as all the other waves had, but in the middle of the bay. It was bigger than the wave Kimo and I had paddled over in '74, a lot bigger. The crest heaved skyward and came straight down on us, closing out the entire bay in one giant section.

Time seemed to stand still for a brief instant. I thought of how much I had accomplished out there. I thought about how I had been the first person to ride inside the tube of Waimea in '77 and all the tube rides I had gotten since then. No one else had done that yet. I figured I was the best there was at this game, and yet here was this wave, this undeniable mass of water, coming to collect its dues for all I had accomplished. This definitely was not supposed to be happening.

As I dove off my board I didn't really know if I could swim under a wave that big, but I knew I had to try. I swam down below the surface as far as I could until the water became dark and my ears started to hurt. I felt the crest of the wave impact above me, like a depth charge sending shock waves through the ocean. They say that wave shook the ground on the beach when it broke. I must have been pretty deep, because it passed over me and I swam to the surface with no turbulence.

"My God! We're all still alive!" was my first thought as I saw Alec, Mark and J.P. pop up in the foaming soup behind me. Mark still had his board. Miraculously, his 24-foot leash had survived. I wasn't using a leash. Alec's and J.P.'s had snapped. Our boards were gone.

ALEC COOKE
PLUCKED FROM WAIMEA'S GNASHING JAWS
PHOTO: DARRELL JONES

A window into the soul of the world's best surfer, provided by close friend and prolific contributor Matt George.

TOM CURREN
PHOTO: MATT GEORGE

Volume 26 | Number 8

THE PRIVATE WORLD OF TOM CURREN

BY MATT GEORGE

1/29/85, 6:02 P.M.

The late January sun is already singing its way over the edge as a small gray truck pulls into Rincon's deserted upper lot. The evening sky is aflame. The car door opens, and a young man dressed in white sweats and a tank top steps out onto the gravel. Arms akimbo, he pauses and looks east toward the purple hues. A moment. Then he begins walking across the lawn toward the cliff stairs, rubbing warmth into his arms against the chill. His walk is reckless but has a hint of purpose. His hair is a tousled dirty blond. He is barefoot.

Down on the beach, he and the sunset are alone. Feet crunch through the low-tide sand crust as he paces out an estimated 100 yards. A simple line is drawn with a scarred heel. Then three deep breaths before he crouches down into a sprinter's start and stares at that piece of driftwood 12 seconds away. His concentration wavers; he is leaving for Costa Rica in the morning. He is going to see his dad for the first time in more than two years. Tomorrow Pat and Tom Curren, father and son, will be out in the lefts of a private ranch point, both doing what they do best. Together. Again. He wonders what it will be like. Then the thoughts focus, the body tenses. He is waiting for that moment.

BANG!

He explodes up and out, urging, forcing himself into the violent rhythm of his first sprint. He's breathing, six seconds, seven seconds, breathing, nine, ten, then the last mad effort, achievement and the warmth of winding it down. Tom comes to a stop, shakes it off, feels pretty good and readies for his next.

Facing the red glow of the west, he crouches.

Marie will be with him, of course. It should be a nice vacation for her, being goofyfoot and all. Thank heaven she and Dad get along so famously. And no wetsuits in the middle of winter is always nice.

BANG!

Three seconds, four, OUCH! Six, seven, breath-ing, stepped on something, nine, ten, pain, can't think about that right now, eleven, twelve. It's over; it's over; control it; take it down.

He checks his toe. Dammit, piece of glass. Not bad, though. Three to go. There is a song playing in his head. The Who, "Sparks." Live version.

In the dark dusk, he readies for sprint number three. Thoughts: He has never surfed Waimea. His dad has. Where does he fit? It was different for Dad. It was physical, more personal. Some glorious mad dedication to massive waves. He remembers what his father said it took to ride the hills: "a lot of rail, and a lot of guts . . ." and how. Chasing that demon out in the thin air, all the right stuff. Him?

BANG!

Three seconds, four, breathing, seven, eight, breathing labored, legs pumping, ten, eleven, ahhh, thirteen, fourteen! He gulps, lousy start, a look at the watch. A slow one. Can't allow that. He thinks about kicking the sand. He doesn't. Number four. All right. This is the one. He crouches again into a start position and remembers:

The first glimpse he had of his father surfing Waimea was with a popcorn in his hand staring at *Goin' Surfin'* flickering across the Vet's Hall too-small screen. Epic Pat Curren footage. To this day, it looks impossible. Is it? Can it be done again . . . ? No, not with that . . . Spirit. It will take something different this time around.

BANG!

Sand flies, three seconds, four, breathing, c'mon, c'mon, five, six, breathing, push it! Eight, nine, now! Ten, eleven, ahhh. Yes! Fast stop. He plops down on his seat and drinks the air. He recov-ers quickly. Better, good.

Tom stands up, looks toward the sea. It's been blown out for two days. A marginal left crumbles in, and Tom imagines himself surfing it. It closes out. He sighs and turns to toe the line. This is number five, the last one, then home. Readying, more thoughts. Costa Rica...he needs this. He decides he wants it. It will be a nice vacation anyway...a sigh. He looks at his toes for a time, eyes fixed, and raises his head as the answer forms: take it as it comes. It's dark now as Tom pads his way up the stairs and over to his car. He feels better for the sprints. It's getting him closer to his goal of never again being fatigued after a competition wave. The cardiovascu-lar advantage, a newfound competition key. A glance at his watch puts a hurry in his step, another glance, a jog. Tom has just remembered something as he hops in the car, and it gives him a good excuse to spin the tires and punch it all the way home.

Marie will have dinner by now, and he's going to be late for that interview. . . .

2/26/85, 6:16 P.M.

On another empty stretch of beach, just south of his beloved Rincon, Tom Curren has just finished stretching out. Australia is for tomorrow. It was great to see his father again. A lot of answers. Confidence is high. He grabs some sand and hour-glasses it through both hands. His father had had his time, made his mark and now lives a simple existence in a foreign land. Now it is Tom's turn. He says his father is quietly impressed by what he's achieved in his career as a pro surfer but that "he laughs at the obligations that come with it."

He stands up and walks over to his starting line. Highway 101 roars to his left; the ocean answers to the right. Tom crouches down. Deaf to it all. Ready. His plan is simple.

A definite structure toward the world crown in 1986 and beyond, a decade of competition, and then take Marie, move to France and live happily ever after.

Have his time, make his mark, and then live a simple existence in a foreign land.

A legacy fulfilled . . . Tommy Curren's way.

BANG!

Two seconds, three, breathing . . . breathing. . . .

Pro surfing's low-water mark or classic surfing theater? The wave-pool event in Allentown, Pennsylvania, was a little bit of both.

Volume 26 | Number 11

NOTES FROM THE DEEP END

BY MATT WARSHAW

June is a good month to be in Pennsylvania. Full-strength heat and humidity come later in the summer season. The drive from Philadelphia to the Allentown area was lovely; dense green foliage, forestlike, cool and shaded, lined a two-lane highway, the Schuylkill River languidly following along on the right. Occasionally, a residence, elegant and old, would be set in a clearing along the road on our left. Allentown itself, and particularly the surrounding area, was just as pleasant.

The local people, moreover, were courteous and friendly. Perhaps a little unsure of what to expect from their visitors, surfboard-laden rent-a-cars being driven slightly in excess of the speed limit, whisking about tan groups of boys with curious accents. One cultural pairing, not at all indicative of the norm, was classic: Kong, caught and absolutely guilty of being too close to the edge of the pool, was being soundly tongue-lashed by a tiny police-boy, one of the poolside authorities, of perhaps 19 years. Kong, evidently, along with an interested group of Aussies, didn't understand the gravity of the situation, and as the little police-boy got angrier, disbelieving smiles (or perhaps patronizing—he was so very tiny) couldn't be concealed. Finally, he challenged Kong: "All right, fine, c'mon—take the first swing!" Kong would have nothing to do with that, and just stood where he was, still smiling. The little police-boy finally wheeled around and stomped off in search of higher authority, turned over his shoulder and shouted, "That's it! You're off the tour!"

All in all, however, the interaction between natives and visitors was quite friendly. At the lifeguard party, as a matter of fact, on the second night of the contest, the ideological and philosophical exchange was . . . hot, as Rambo would have put it. . . .

. . . The sun was dropping. It was an hour after the final had ended. The machine was off, and almost everyone, onlookers and contestants, had trailed into the parking lot and driven away. South Africa, and with it a whole new series of questions, lay before the ASP's touring professionals.

The surfers had enjoyed themselves. It was something so totally different it couldn't really miss. Indelibly etched into my mind, and perhaps one of the all-time great lighthearted moments in pro surfing history, occurred during a break in the Main Event Saturday. The pool had opened to the public for a half hour, and there mingling with the 100 or so of Allentown's more adventurous citizens, were three-quarters of the top 25 surfers in the world, all riding rented Boogie Boards and having a blast.

Still, by Sunday evening, everyone just wanted to go surfing. In real waves. Behind the pool, Tommy Carroll answered questions from two or three reporters from the local press, diplomatically fielding queries on the pool itself; the camaraderie among surfers; life on the road. Stock stuff. When asked to compare the pool to big ocean waves, though, The Champ momentarily became animated. "If I could show you what happens when a wave gives you some real speed . . . !" He haltingly, but with feeling, described dropping into 12-foot Sunset, the power and the adrenaline. He smiled at the reporters and finished, "It would blow you away."

ALLENTOWN, PENNSYLVANIA
SURF'S UP—AND SAFE—AT DORNEY PARK
PHOTO: MATT GEORGE

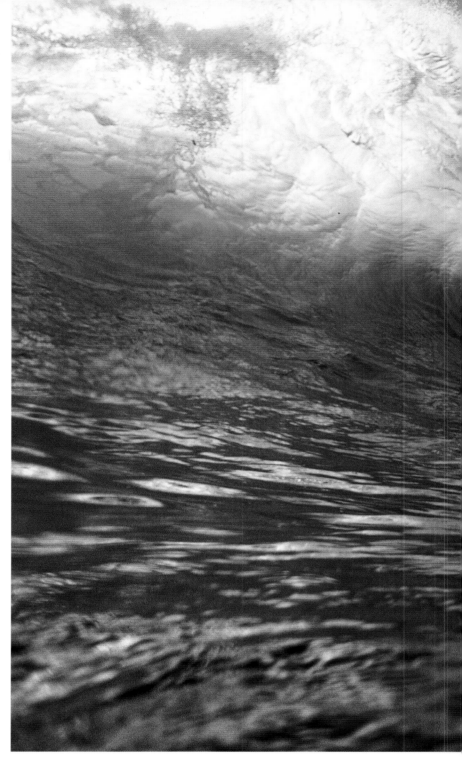

"HARBOR BILL" MULCOY
PHOTO: WOODY WOODWORTH

Despite the increasingly homogenized versions of surfing heroes being served up by the media, there were still a few rebels out there.

Volume 27 | *Number 7*

SAGA OF SAFE HARBOR BILL

BY MATT GEORGE

THE PROBLEM

Harbormaster Steve Scheiblauer leaned against his office window, steaming coffee mug in hand, and sighed deeply. He had a problem. A big problem. Its name was a shadow known only as "Harbor Bill." This "Harbor Bill" had moved to the forefront of the ongoing battle between the Santa Cruz Harbor Patrol and the surfers who illegally ride the waves at the harbor's entrance. Scheiblauer had the Army Corps of Engineers to thank for that; it was their construction blunder years ago that caused the dramatic shoaling off the west jetty in the first place. For the surfers, the resulting sandbar meant a perfect winter wave. For the boat owner, it meant a recurring winter nightmare—a gauntlet of ocean violence to be run at every outing. Or barricading the entrance completely, damming them in like so many beavers.

But all that didn't matter now. Laws had been passed; Scheiblauer had a job to do. He must arrest "Harbor Bill" for surfing the entrance and breaking the law. A scapegoat? Maybe. But then sometimes that's just another name for a leader.

The harbormaster tested his coffee and eyed his jurisdiction, a rather quaint harbor setting, and for a moment wished there was a way for everyone to cooperate. Being a surfer himself, he respected a great many of them as good watermen and had an understanding of their independent nature. Indeed, their knowledge of the ocean had resulted in saved lives at the entrance when inexperienced boat owners had foundered and broached and become helpless. He'd seen it with his own eyes. But cooperation was out of the question; so was any real communication. They'd tried both and a small group of ill-mannered surfers had blown that tactic. And it had come time for the patrol to do their duty: uphold the law.

Another sigh. It bugged him a little that this one guy had been so elusive and had escaped arrest so many times. This character actually had a following, like some surfing Robin Hood. Apprehended surfers staunchly refused to give his name, and civilians had gone so far as to cheer and aid his escapes on a number of occasions. A recent one in particular. . . .

THE X-FACTOR

Harbormaster Scheiblauer shook his head slowly. There had been so many other times. They lost him once when he ran down the beach and paddled out under the wharf into huge surf. Another time he had buried his board in the sand up on the beach and casually walked past the very officers who were looking for him. And there was even some wild rumor that he had hid among a rookery of seals off Steamer Lane until the coast was clear. The public loved that one. Hell, they loved him. Who was this guy anyway? Did he even have a name?

Scheiblauer turned from the picture window and sat at his desk. It was early yet, still time to peruse the morning mail. He was stoked when he saw the new issue of SURFER had arrived, positively elated when he found that it featured an article on Santa Cruz. Then suddenly, as he turned to page 83, he froze in his chair as the answer to the problem jumped up and slapped him awake. . . .

The paragraph read, "Or maybe the Harbormouth, that million-dollar wave,

and the kind of place where legends are made in a day. Pat O'Neill's frighteningly late drops are still talked about, and 'Harbor Bill' Mulcoy's local knowledge of the place allows him heroism five times a day."

There it was in black and white. His name. "Harbor Bill" Mulcoy.

The harbormaster's adversary had just assumed an identity. And a hastily snatched city directory provided all that was needed for the arrest. He sat there and looked at it again. In one instant of sheer chance, the thorn in his side had been cleanly plucked. And it wasn't until he sat back and calmly finished his coffee that Harbormaster Steve Scheiblauer reached for the phone. . . .

At exactly 3:50 p.m. on June 14, 1985, William John Mulcoy, 37, a golf course groundskeeper, a husband, a father, a surfer, walked into the harbormaster's office to, as it states in the official report, "face the music." After 14 years of play, the game was up.

Pro surfing in America never fully recovered from the infamous Op Pro party riot.

Volume 28 | Number 1

WINNERS AND LOSERS

BY MATT WARSHAW

D. David Morin really is a solid, right-on announcer: witty, charming and very professional—sort of the Vince Scully of surf broadcasting. Which made it all the more bizarre, during the final minutes of competition at the 1986 Op Pro, when D. David cheerfully asked the crowd, "All right, how many people think this is the best Op we've ever had?"—while directly behind him, about 50 feet away as the bottle flies, a straight-up, Watts-on-the-sand riot was in progress.

The 11 o'clock news that night called it "full-scale." In front of the lifeguard headquarters—a hundred yards from the con-

HUNTINGTON MOB
PHOTO: JEFF DIVINE

test's southern grandstand—three police cars, a lifeguard Jeep, a police van, a beach ambulance and an ATC three-wheeler were burned up, smashed up, or both. Two of the cars were flipped over. Engine parts from the torched cars had been torn out and thrown through the headquarters' windows. Soot from the burned autos blackened rows and rows of cars in the parking lot north of the

headquarters, and some of the cars there had been vandalized. Inside the garage, there was a bullet hole in the ceiling where Marine Safety Captain Bill Richardson—the only man not to flee the headquarters when it appeared the rioters would storm in—had fired a warning shot at a group who had gained entrance.

By the time D. David asked the crowd if this was the best Op they'd ever seen, however, the action had moved away from the lifeguard area and was actually raging on directly behind the judges' scaffolding. There, police in riot gear faced off against a semi-crazed mob of perhaps 5,000, a hundred or so of whom were throwing bottles, cans and rocks—anything they could get their hands on.

The trouble had started about an hour earlier when police tried to assist two women who flashed some skin (by choice or force is up for speculation). The officers were showered with bottles and rocks, beat a hasty retreat and sent for reinforcements. From that point on, the violence slowly magnified, hitting a crescendo with the car-burning, but still was heated when the contest was over.

The ignorance, stupidity, and ugliness of the whole scene—the absolute pointlessness—was numbing. And having the riot working perversely in tandem with the men's final—the very climax of the Op Pro—just added to the feeling of surreal weirdness.

POSTSCRIPT ONE: A two-and-a-half-hour town council meeting was held Sept. 2, two days after the Op Pro, during which the vast majority of speakers (including Huntington mayor Robert P. Mandic, Jr.) indicated that the Op Pro may be run next year, pending certain changes: removing the contest from Labor Day weekend, separating the surfing from the bikini contest and the skateboard exhibition, and charging admission were some of the points brought up.

Sue Chisolm, promotions director for Ocean Pacific, later said that "Op will be putting on a surfing contest next year; we just don't know where or when. Hopefully in California."

POSTSCRIPT TWO: The television clips aired following the riot showed one particularly repugnant scene: as an overturned police car burned out of control, a rioter got hold of a lifeguard ATC three-wheeler, ghost-rode it into the fire, turned around and raised both arms in triumph.

Returning to the scene of his crime the next day, he told the story to a nice-looking girl standing nearby—trying to make an impression before asking her out. She agreed to see him, asked for his name and phone number, said goodbye . . . and went directly to a nearby police officer. The man was arrested and booked within the hour.

MARK FOO
*CHASING HIS ULTIMATE
DESTINY AT WAIMEA BAY*
PHOTO: DARRELL JONES

**Big-wave rider Mark Foo contemplated mortality,
eerily predicting his own end eight years later.**

Volume 28 | *Number 2*

THE ULTIMATE THRILL

BY MATT WARSHAW

DO YOU EVER THINK ABOUT DYING RIDING BIG WAVES?
Well, kinda, but . . . I mean, I'm not afraid of dying in that situation. You have to understand that if you want the ultimate thrill, you've got to be willing to pay the ultimate price.

Also, to me it's not tragic to die doing something you love. It's like the shuttle astronauts. I mean, when they died—as much of a tragedy as it was—you have to consider that for them, they were doing what they had geared their whole lives to do. They were at the climax of that, and it's not a bad way to go, if you gotta go. I don't have a death wish or anything, but I could die happy today. I've had it pretty good.

But at the same time, part of the reason I'm not afraid is because I've survived situations where I could have died. So I know I'm a survivor.

Sponsored by this communist country's Olympic Committee, SURFER's groundbreaking trip to China reasserted the notion that surfing's party line was more than mere sport.

Volume 28 | Number 6

BEYOND THE GREAT WALL

BY MATT GEORGE

I was thinking about this at the moment the sun baked into us: It seemed a perfect time to reflect on our entire experience here in China. We would be leaving tonight, and left behind us would be this completely isolated microcosm of surf spirit. One that has never existed so exotically in all the world. It made all my impressions about the significance of our presence in China a jumble, so I abandoned them. And I decided instead to hope that despite all the thousands of changes, influences and beliefs that the modern world was pressing into China, the simple spirit of surfing would somehow survive. . . .

Off on a small muddy rise—at a fork in the trail that led to his land—a farmer and his son stood side by side. The shad-

ows of the late day were long cast by an imposing sun that hung just above the horizon. A mean mosquito dusk would soon fall. The farmer was a man in his prime whose life of toil had twisted him into a bundle of ligaments and hard, ropy muscle. His son was a 12-year-old version of the same. They were both watching an automobile make its way off to the north for the last time, pulling a little cloud of dust behind it. The Americans who were in that automobile had been taking this farmer's son into the sea for the last few days and teaching him sport. So many changes had been coming to this land, the farmer thought. So many temptations for the young to explore. Tomorrow didn't exist anymore, only today. It made him wonder about the future for his son, so he

took comfort in some words from the Tao te ching:

**Chasing the beasts of the field
will drive a man mad.
The goods that are hard to procure
are hobbles that slow walking feet.
But the wise man will do what
his belly dictates,
and never the sight of his eyes.
Thus he will choose this and not that. . . .**

By now, the automobile was beyond sight. So the man turned and started his walk home with his hand on the back of his son's neck. And all he could think of as he made his way through the mud was that it was going to take days to get his son's mind back on the tending of the fields. . . .

BRAD GERLACH
PRACTICES HIS STAND-UP
ROUTINE IN CARLSBAD
PHOTO: ROB GILLEY

**California's Brad Gerlach
was loud and living proof that
surfing breeds characters.**

Volume 28 | Number 8

TALK SHOW

He hasn't been in the water in two days, and he doesn't think he'll get in tomorrow. He just feels a little burned out; it'll pass. But for the time being, Brad Gerlach doesn't care to talk about surfing. A routine discussion about diet and training is interrupted with him saying, "I want to talk about more offbeat stuff. I want to get this thing rolling."

He's just not exactly sure what it is he wants to talk about. . . .

DESCRIBE YOUR IDEA OF THE PERFECT GIRL.

She's got to be rugged. I want a girl I can rough around with. Where I could say, "Let's go climb something high. Here, carry this," and she wouldn't snivel. She's got to speak her mind, and she's got to have a good sense of humor.

LOOKS?

I like brown-haired girls. I like blonde-haired girls, too, but I like brown-haired girls more. And long hair. I hate short hair; I don't think I've ever gone out with a girl with short hair. I like 'em rugged, but I like 'em feminine.

I don't know what it is exactly, but I like Latin girls. Just a touch of Latin. It's a sultry look.

I like a girl who's well-toned and almost as tall as me. And I'm not out of the '60s: I don't like big, huge tits. That just doesn't cut it. Of course, when I was younger, they didn't go unappreciated. I like firm apples. Like, say, Washington apples.

SO WHAT WOULD A DREAM DATE WITH BRAD GERLACH BE LIKE?

A dream date with Brad Gerlach. Let's see. Well, first of all, I want to make this clear: I'm not a growler. It's not like, "There's another one," and pounce. I'm not a sleaze, and there's a lot of guys on the tour who are—I want to name names, but I can't. I'm not a one-night-stand guy. I used to be 'cause of peer pressure, but not anymore. That blows girls away sometimes, because they expect me to grip 'em, and I don't. I like to flow. And besides, that stuff's dangerous these days.

SO YOU'RE NOT A GROWLER. YOU CAN STILL HAVE A DREAM DATE.

OK [pauses for a moment]. Well, I think it would start out just driving somewhere really fast. Me and my date in my new car. As fast as it could go, like 140 or 150. Headed for...I don't know. Headed for the desert. To some kind of small nightclub; nothing hip or trendy. And there's all kinds of people there, warm people, people who don't know me. Or if they know me, it's not like, "Oh, wow, it's Brad Gerlach." None of that kind of stuff. It's just really friendly; it's totally happening, and as soon as we get out of the car, the first person we see yells out, "All right! How you doing?" And from that point, we're on a roll.

SO YOU GO INSIDE THE CLUB.

So we go inside the club, and she branches out; she's off doing her own thing, and I'm talking to the boys. Then I'm back with her, and we're dancing, and they're just playing the killer music. Killer dance music.

And then...shit, I don't know. It's hard for me to plan these things; they just happen.

No, OK, then we'd meet someone there at the club, and they'd suggest something to do, and a group of us would be all, "Yeah! Let's do it!" and we're off. Like we'd go slide down a hill on a big piece of cardboard or something.

So we're doing this, and we're doing that. It's never [in a slow, bored voice], "So...what do you want to do now?" It's constant movement. We'd drive to Vegas. We'd gamble a bit and win a lot of money. We're on a roll. We'd get married, then shine it on a couple hours later. Just for a joke.

Then we'd buy skis and equipment and go to Aspen for a couple days, staying in a cabin on a hill. And the only thing in the living room is a fireplace and a killer stereo. Like a $10,000 stereo system. Music's key.

And then we'd fly to Key West to get a tan. Then we'd just keep on cruising. We're on a roll, still.

My dream date could actually go on for months.

MARK OCCHILUPO
ON TOP OF THE WORLD . . .
OR AT LEAST CRONULLA
PHOTO: MATT GEORGE

Matt George's intimate profile provided a glimpse beneath the shine of Mark Occhilupo's rising star.

MARK OCCHILUPO
BACKSIDE POWER SURFING AT ITS BEST
PHOTO: JEFF DIVINE

Volume 28 | Number 11

COMING OF AGE

BY MATT GEORGE / ART BY GLENN CHASE

The train finally arrived, although a bit late, and emptied its harried commuters. Mark hopped out of the car, called out once, and then met a man in the street you would never guess was his father: a tall, dark, very Italian-looking man with jet-black, neatly combed hair. Mark hugged his father briefly, then opened the passenger door for him before walking around to get behind the wheel. As I met the head of the family, it became clear that he'd had a long day. We drove for a while, headed for the outskirts toward Kurnell, where the family home is. There was an obvious air of respect for Luciano Occhilupo, the civil engineer.

Mark began a conversation with him: "So, Daddy, what did you think of the contest yesterday, eh?"

"Pretty good, pretty good," his father replied with reserve. "But how come you fall off with Carroll many times?"

A cloud crossed Mark's brow, but he answered simply, slightly resigned: "Aw, yeah…I know. I fell off on the easy parts, too, eh, Daddy?"

"Yes, you deserve to lose twice for that—for that surfing."

His sister Fleur came to his rescue at this point, asking Luciano about his day. But the tension remained on Mark's face, and he was pretty quiet after that, smacking his lips softly and keeping his eyes on the road.

The dinner was marvelous: a vegetarian feast. Mark's proud mother, a charming New Zealander, was the perfect hostess. Mark is the youngest child, the only boy, and is treated with unabashed adoration by his three sisters and his mom. It's a tight family unit—what one would call "a good home." It was a pleasant evening, in contrast to the previous night's howler, even though Mark remained preoccupied throughout.

Later on, during the drive back to Cronulla, Fleur reached up from the backseat, placed her hand on Mark's arm, and said, "Don't worry, Mark, that's just the way he shows you he cares." Mark smiled vaguely at this and drove on in silence, his eyebrows raised.

By midnight, Mark's apartment was quiet. Having rolled out of bed for a drink of water, I now stood alone in his darkened living room pressed up against the picture window, looking out to sea. Standing there nose to nose with my own reflection made me think of what Mark had said down by the ocean's edge. A sort of answer to that was slowly coming to me. It seems that until recently, life had just happened to Mark; he had simply played the cards he'd been dealt. That would explain his feelings of disbelief as he stood surrounded and baffled by "the benefits that have been given to me for surfing well." And that it was all so "unbelievable, really." But now…now it felt as if he was on some personal threshold.

Mark's incredible natural talent had afforded him wealth and greatness in this world, and perhaps for the first time in his life, he'd begun to question that. ("But it is me, isn't it?") Maybe at 20 years of age, Mark Occhilupo was losing an innocence and no longer considered that fate was his stage manager. His sincere passion for surfing—something he's only beginning to articulate—his world championship goal and the motives behind it…that much seemed to fit.

But something was still missing. I could feel it tonight especially. He seemed unsettled almost…dissatisfied. As I looked around at some of the evidence of his success—the Pipe Masters' trophy, the new home and its Camelot viewpoint overlooking the ocean in his hometown of Cronulla—it made me wonder why. What more was he trying to figure out?

The dentist's drill had been whining steadily for more than an hour before Mark Occhilupo came staggering into the waiting room. His mouth was stuffed with cotton wadding. I asked him how it went in there. He just groaned and plopped a strange object into my hand. I looked down. It was the enormous, blood-stained molar that he'd just had removed, along with getting six new fillings. Since the surf was flat that morning, he'd decided to get it taken care of while he could. He was taking all of this in pretty good stride.

We returned to his apartment and he stretched out on the couch, making jokes about the pain in his jaw. The sunlight spilled in generously as we lounged around entertaining thoughts of an evening glass-off.

Mark soon became introspective, and after a while said, "Hey, mate, pretty heavy with my father last night, eh?" I agreed, yes.

He replied, "It's really funny, you know? How females don't understand at all the relationship between a father and son. How we feel like we can never satisfy them." I agreed again. Yes, it is funny.

He continued, "Well, I'm glad you were there to see all that. It really gives me a chance to say something I've wanted to say for a while now, and I think it has a lot to do with this." He sat up and took the bloody gauze out of his mouth, holding it in his right hand.

"Well, mate, I'm sure you noticed that my father is a very Italian-looking man. In this country, they have a name for that. They don't like immigrants— they call them 'Wogs.' I guess it's like calling a black person in America something terrible. Well, I really used to be embarrassed about that—that I was a 'Wog,' you know? I used to hide in school, wanted to change my name and all that. I think my dad knew."

He took a deep breath here, collecting himself. "Well, the Coke Contest was one of the first times my father has ever come to watch me surf, and when I saw him there off to the side, all of a sudden I didn't feel that way anymore. I have achieved some things now, and…I was proud of family, my heritage. My dad has done a lot for me. I mean, I even have his name. My name is Marco Luciano J. Occhilupo…I guess that's who I am now."

I said I thought I understood what he was talking about, and with that, Marco Luciano J. Occhilupo laid back, looking satisfied, and was shortly fast asleep.

CHEYNE HORAN
INCESSANT INNOVATION, OFF THE WALL
PHOTOS: JEFF DIVINE

HORAN
*FOUR-TIME WORLD-TITLE RUNNER-UP,
BUT A MAJOR FORCE IN ANY OUTFIT*
PHOTO: JEFF DIVINE

Continuing his series of revealing character studies, Matt George got close to Cheyne Horan, one of the 1980s' most talented—and troubled—personalities.

Volume 29 | *Number 4*

CHEYNE HORAN'S RAINBOW BRIDGE

BY MATT GEORGE

Kerry, Brad and Paul are all hugging their knees at this point, staring into the center of our circle. Cheyne sits cross-legged, bolt upright. More enchantment is needed; Cocker is singing "Feeling Alright." I asked Cheyne what he would transform the world into. What exactly needed this "fixing up."

"What needs fixing up?" he asked, surprised that I didn't know the answer. "Well…people are starving; we've got a nuclear threat hanging over our heads every day—there's that paranoia. There's f---in' shit in the ocean . . . and after all that is fixed up, that'll clean up the vibration, and then the relationships between leaders can be fixed up. . . ."

What kind of fixing up do these relationships need, Cheyne?

He takes a breath and comes down a bit. "I reckon just harmony, basically. . . ."

Kerry is on it now. "It's like…yoga is sort of an integration. You know that in the body there are seven centers?"

No, I replied, I didn't know that.

"Well," he explained, "the kundalini, which is the yoga we practice, is sort of a male/female bond of that multi-structure. And the idea is to awaken it and pierce all those centers in the middle of your body until it hits your head. Enlightenment, and all that sort of stuff." Kerry went on to explain that everyone is split into two polarities: male and female. The problem is that no one has this figured out, really. The answer is to seek a way to even out these male and female polarities—the yin and yang—so they cancel each other out and transform the individual into a more complete, balanced person. We gotta fix this up first.

Does this fixing up require a bisexual lifestyle, then? I asked. Dead silence. The music had stopped. Everyone was waiting for Kerry to field that one.

He eventually does. "OK, we're a yoga group. And at the moment, we're a celibate yoga group. Everyone has to handle their sexuality in their own way. But we're a tantra yoga group eventually, too.

Tantra yoga involves centering yourself through touch. It's actually through touching or using sexuality as an engine to find the kundalini centers. It's a high and advanced yoga. . . ."

I ponder this. Everyone is pondering this. I turn to Cheyne and look him in the eyes. Cheyne? I ask, in the quiet. Is that the way you feel about all this, too?

He hesitates, and then answers, gently. "Yeah . . . that's right. That's, um . . . that's how I feel about it, too. . . ."

By this time, the peripheral effects of all the enchantment going on had made me about as high as a kite. Paul had just dozed off, and Brad lay on his back, tapping his hands against his chest to the beat of a song in his head. Kerry had begun explaining just how easy it would be for the world to be harmonized through "global enchantment," and Cheyne? Cheyne remained cross-legged, still bolt upright, staring deeply into a full-length mirror that was propped up over by the barbells. His posture was so intent, so wise, yet the look on his face as he peered into his own eyes seemed so naive. Twenty-six years old, I thought. Twenty-six. It made me wonder just what he was seeing. . . .

Cheyne and I were sitting up on the chimney rock that overlooks the pass; Byron Bay's famous point. He was in the process of dropping me off in town. It was time for both of us to start thinking about getting down to Bells. We'd decided to check the surf first. It was sparkling in at 2 feet, pipedream perfect, with a raft of silhouette figures moving about in the lineup's diamond field reflections. We were flanked by the enormous, verdant headland. The utter beauty of the scene right there, right then, was astounding. We were alone. I could tell Cheyne had something to say for himself.

He got it. "I'm not a homosexual. That's not the way it is. . . ." I just nodded. He continued. "A lot of this prejudice I get on the tour is just people and their assumptions. I've been treated as a homosexual, but that's not me. I love women . . . I'm just into modifying my sincerity right now,

learning about myself. That's why I'm celibate. Because, when I choose someone to love, it will be because I am complete, and able to touch and share with purity. [pause] I know people get uptight about my trip—my yoga, my friends, my ideas. I just take that as it comes. . . . No one really knows me. My mystique is there, though, because I'm still out there battling on the front lines, still surfing against the best in the world on my own terms, and I just won't go away."

A bigger set moved through. We watched it tumble in—the whole thing. When it was over, I mentioned that maybe there had been a lot of assumptions because Kerry sometimes did a lot of talking for him.

Cheyne said, "No . . . no. He makes things a lot clearer than I can make them for people. I'm practicing the stuff. I'm in an initiation stage, and he's the leader of the group. I have my own voice, but it's an internal voice. It's not a struggle, either—it's like an understanding. And one of the things I understand is that I don't care what people think of me. I know me; my friends know me . . . that's enough for me, I think."

I asked him what was coming up for him, short term.

"Well, my . . . extremism has got me on the edge with my sponsors right now. If that doesn't get any better, I won't have any backing. You can't do anything without backing. I'll be a. . . . Look, I love pro surfing, mate. I wish I could be mentally and physically able to compete until I was 46."

But, I had to mention, this year was the second year in a row that his Top 16 seed was seriously in question. What would happen, I asked, if he dropped out of the Top 16?

At this, he turned his head, brow furrowed, and stared down at his feet, picking at his toes. Another set moved through. He didn't watch this one. He just waited a bit, suddenly looked up at a seagull pin-wheeling overhead, and replied, "I can't even think about that. . . ."

Pro surfer/shaper Dave Parmenter was developing as one of pro surfing's most vocal critics—and one of the sport's most eloquent spokesmen.

Volume 30 | *Number 2*

ICONOCLAST NOW

BY DAVE PARMENTER

The state of the art in professional surfing has become bored as hell. The Holy Grail now is just hitting the lip. Oh, sure, the ASP has added power and speed to its little rule book, but that's lip service; most surfers are still just surfing off their fins with no regard to burying a rail. On the tour there are Tom Curren, Tom Carroll, Mark Occhilupo, Martin Potter and that's it. No one else even comes close. The only way these guys can be beaten is if they make a mistake. They are never outsurfed. That's impossible. It's easy to see how a guy like Tom Curren or Occy could get bored with that. I know I would be. These guys are the best we've got, and we're boring them.

What about the others? There are some hot surfers out there, but the majority of this New Breed aren't even good enough to know any better. This power and speed thing is just lip service, because there's still so much noncommittal surfing going on—so much flapping and slapping; so much counterproductive body movement. Surfing used to be the art of making difficult maneuvers look easy. Do that now and you're all washed up. You have to make incredibly easy things look hard. You have to do recovery maneuvers—flop-over-and-stand-back-up cutbacks—then raise a clenched fist to the sky with your eyes rolled back in exaltation . . . God!

What effect is this having on the next generation? Are you kidding? Where do I start? Look, pro surfing has become the heaviest influence on kids today, only they can't see that a lot of it is just like the emperor's new clothes. The amateur scene is pathetic. These kids don't have a clue. They're growing up baited with all these crazy incentives so they can be brainwashed into being "the next Tom Curren"—which is the most trotted-out cliché I can think of. They're missing out completely. It's all stickers and freebies. Now their first sponsorship is put right up there with losing their virginity, for God's sake. It's all about incentives, not participation. It's about following the Holy Bible of Tom Curren's blueprint—of doing it the way he did. They aren't even given the chance to realize that Curren hardly had anything to do with what amateur surfing offered. I mean, he just sailed through it on sheer genius. He was like one of those kids who goes through school and never has to do his homework until he's on the bus. These new kids are handed this phantom blueprint and talked into working it over and over like some mine that has long since been depleted of its minerals. In the meantime, they're missing out on surfing. Competing is just a tiny sliver of what surfing has to offer, but to these kids, it's become a material quest. And surfing is not a material quest . . . it's a spiritual quest.

Mickey Dora was back with this cryptic tale, leading off with the Dark Knight's first allusion to his 1984 prison sentence and ending, some 10,000 words later, in the deserts of Namibia.

Volume 30 | Number 7

MILLION DAYS TO DARKNESS

BY MICKEY DORA / ART BY THE PIZZ

WERE YOU EVER IN THE MILITARY?
No.

DID YOU EVER SERVE IN ANY OTHER ARMED FORCES?
No.

DID YOU EVER WORK FOR THE GOVERNMENT?
No.

DO YOU OWN ANY PROPERTY?
No.

DO YOU HAVE A HOME?
No.

DO YOU HAVE ANY INSURANCE OR A PENSION?
No.

DO YOU HAVE A BANK ACCOUNT OR CREDIT CARD?
No.

HAVE YOU EVER BEEN ON WELFARE OR FOOD STAMPS?
Nope.

DO YOU OWN ANYTHING?
No.

HAVE YOU EVER BEEN MARRIED?
Nope.

ARE YOU HOMOSEXUAL?
Isn't everybody in this screwed-up country?

WHO THE HELL DO YOU THINK YOU ARE?
Who the hell do you want me to be?

JUST ANSWER THE QUESTION. YES OR NO? HOW DO YOU MAKE YOUR LIVING?
By the oldest of livelihoods, free trade.

NOW WHAT THE HELL WOULD THAT BE?
Barter.

YOU'RE A LIAR! YOU'RE TRAFFICKING IN DRUGS. YOU OWE THE IRS $300,000. CASE CLOSED.
To quote Faustus: "Youth and debauchery are magnificent, but eventually you have the Devil to pay."

Stripped naked, I stood there manacled, shackled and chained, like any other slave caught in the 20th century, where human beings are trapped, brainwashed and otherwise destroyed by a mindless disciplinary process.

No Amnesty International or bogus Helsinki Accord.

With everything I owned confiscated, I was tossed a government-issue jumpsuit accompanied by the inevitable standard caustic remark, "Hey, man, what's your beef?"

With one of my particularly favorite prosaic façade expressions, I responded, "Among other things, improper abuse of credit."

A few of the local homeboys were checking me out as if I were a two-bit purse snatcher. One blurted out, "Oh, yeah, went to Vegas for the weekend, huh?"

In my best diction, I replied, "No, not exactly. Just took a wee trip around the world."

"Huh? Oh, yeah! How long were you gone, man?"

And I was able to make the triumphant declaration: "Seven years, man!"

A loud cheer burst forth as the guard escorted me to my cell: Maximum Security, Terminal Island Federal Penitentiary, Long Beach, California.

KELLY SLATER
NEW SCHOOL LIP-SLIDING IN BAJA
PHOTO: ROB GILLEY

Every new era needs a hero, and by the end of the 1980s, a phenomenal new young talent from Florida stood on the threshold of greatness. Again, Matt George was there to contemplate the ascension.

Volume 30 | *Number 8*

THE SEDUCTION OF KELLY SLATER

BY MATT GEORGE

He sleeps like an angel: curled up on his side, dark eyebrows slightly raised, hugging his pillow to his chin. His adult-looking face, with its startling jade eyes, retired for the day, transformed into childlike repose, numb and divine. A face at peace with a world that is treating him so kindly.

Or, so it would seem. . . .

Leaning against a bare wall in his room, I listened to the sounds of the night: Kelly's measured breathing, the hissing of the nearby Atlantic—its gummy breeze sifting through the palms—and, strangely, the low snorting of two manatees lumbering by in the lagoon system that laces itself through the backyards of sea-level Cocoa Beach.

I glanced at the alarm clock. It was 3 a.m. on a January school night. Kelly and I had been up slumber-party talking, and the conversation had just drifted off. He was gone in a matter of seconds. I was alone with my thoughts.

Now and then, the night wind would lift the tattered sheet that was nailed up over his open window and spirit its way around his room. In one corner were a few split packing boxes, overflowing with trophies. In another was a single chest of drawers. Across the room was a closet with its doors off the hinges, and hanging inside was what looked like a salesman's ultimate sample rack of every surf apparel manufacturer in the business: wetsuits, T-shirts, sweats, the works—most with their tags still dangling. These labels would spin and eddy intermittently, forming a strange-looking mobile. And to my left, on the otherwise naked walls, was the single poster Kelly had tacked up, depicting a cartoon character with its head up its own ass. The slogan read: YOUR PROBLEM IS OBVIOUS.

On the tile floor, Kelly was lying on a mattress with a blanket pulled up to his chin.

The look and feel of this household I'd become a part of a few days earlier had been a surprise to me. Considering Kelly Slater's Golden Child public image, already seasoned by years of advertising, I'd expected something a bit more...well, silver spoon. I found myself oddly pleased it wasn't. There were no pretenses here—this was salt-of-the-earth stuff.

From the moment I walked in the house—a white stucco tract unit—I'd been treated like family. Furthermore, the Slater clan was one of the most easygoing and loving I'd ever come across: mother Judy, a onetime firefighter, bartender, waitress and currently unemployed; stepfather Walker, a marine engine mechanic; older brother Sean and younger brother Steven. The family had been nomadic for three years now, since Judy's divorce from the children's natural father, moving from house to house, keeping a lot of things in boxes. They'd been renting this house for the last six months, but it, too, was up for sale, and rumor had it the Realtor had found a buyer. They'd be moving again soon. No one was quite sure when.

I looked at the clock: 3:05 a.m. Again, the sheet over the window moved. Beyond was what Kelly had referred to as "the whole world out there." Funny how he'd put it that way. As if it were a separate entity, laying in wait, a presence expecting such big things from him.

My impressions of the last five days were coming like still-life photos now, a mosaic of random moments that shed some light on the inner workings of this 17-year-old prodigy sleeping before me.

Chapter Four

The Nineties
New School

In 1990, SURFER assumed a new young editor, Matt Warshaw, a former competitor and perhaps the best surfer yet to man the helm. Good thing—the '90s were going to take some finesse. SURFER had hit an almost frantic stride by the peak of the surf-fashion craze in the early days of the decade. The magazine grew fat and the tone was strident. It was an era of superlatives screaming out from a series of bright covers: "The Best of the '80s," "Deepest Indonesia," "Huge Surf," "Exotic," "Surfin' USA" and "Summer Bash." There were still those elements that maintained a comforting continuity, binding in a chain 1990s issues of SURFER to ones from the 1960s. The photography was stunning, with masters like Brewer, Divine, Servais and Gilley, plus Australians Ted Grambeau and Peter Wilson, still tack-sharp and fresh. New places: Baja's big waves on Isla Todos Santos, Portugal, Java and Tahiti. There was competition, new champions like South Africa's Martin Potter and Hawaii's Derek Ho, and emerging stars of the future, like Florida's Kelly Slater, featured on the cover of the last issue of 1990. Words—some of the best, most sophisticated writing ever by Matt Warshaw, Matt George, sportswriter Bruce Jenkins, Steve Barilotti, Ben Marcus, Derek Hynd and the inimitable surfer/shaper/philosopher Dave Parmenter. Under the glare was the eloquence.

But was SURFER still the voice of surfing? It was hard to tell from all the shouting. Then came the October 1991 issue. Designed by art director Dave Carson, this magazine's look took a 180-degree turn. Carson, an accomplished surfer and artist who was steeped in New York's postmodern nihilist scene, was given free creative rein, and with no warning, the sunny, four-color world of SURFER turned dark and moody. Distressed type, fractured, convoluted body copy, distorted images; the new vision was all shadows and haze. Affectation or disaffection? It was had to tell. Steve Hawk, a former newspaper reporter who took over as SURFER editor (following Warshaw's defection to grad school), felt the surf-publishing scene so complacent as to demand this graphic self-immolation. Response was unprecedented: designers commended the innovation while the rest of the surfing world, unified in zealous derision, howled in outrage, "Give us our magazine back!"

Within months, Carson was gone, and the magazine's traditional palette returned: blue tubes, white spindrift and the golden warmth of the sun. Order was reestablished, but the scare had shaken SURFER's

readers—and its staff. Who would have guessed after all these years that the readership could still feel so intimately connected with "their" magazine? And react so passionately? Who was SURFER preaching to? By the mid-1990s, it was getting harder and harder to tell. Steve Pezman had it easy in the cohesive mid-'70s. SURFER editors in the '90s were faced with a great challenge.

Surfing realities in the '90s were the most diverse the sport had ever known. The growth of longboarding, indicative not only of the aging of the sport but of a palpable shift toward recreational surfing, confused the simple, celebrity-driven marketing strategies of only a few years previous. Women's surfing was on the rise but was given little room editorially, save for a cover featuring World Champion Lisa Andersen, the first female surfer to grace the cover of SURFER since Margo Oberg 15 years before. The advent of motorized "tow-in" surfing rendered obsolete the formerly unassailable appeal of man-against-the-sea, big-wave drama. And it was becoming more and more obvious that the bulk of the surfing world cared little for the vagaries of professional competition. Everybody loved all the pretty pictures, but could SURFER continue to speak to all surfers?

Evan Slater, the last SURFER editor of the 20th century, believed so. Slater, a former professional and renowned big-wave rider, infused the magazine with renewed reverence for the act of surfing, mandating a policy of responsibility—and accountability—through a series of issue-oriented editorial features. Drawing on experienced talent like Dave Parmenter, Sam George and Tim Baker (former editor of Australia's innovative *Tracks* magazine), Slater counteracted the magazine's often elitist tone with both humor and provocative self-examination—Baker's critical essay on pre-packaged international surf adventure exemplifying this new direction.

Then again, perhaps, not so new. In 1960, its founder, John Severson, struggled to find a name for the new magazine. He came up with dozens but finally narrowed his list down to three: *Surfing*, *Surf* and *The Surfer*. Severson went with his third choice—his gut choice. "It was the player," he once wrote. "It was something we were going to do together."

By the end of its 40th year, SURFER had found this voice again. It did so by listening to the same voice John Severson heard so many years ago. The collective voice of those whose magazine this has been and will always be: the surfer.

CLOCKWISE FROM TOP LEFT:

MEGAN ABUBO AND ROCHELLE BALLARD
GIRL STARS
PHOTO: ART BREWER

KELLY SLATER
KING KELLY, FLORIDA,
HOME WATERS
PHOTO: DICK MESEROLL

ROB MACHADO
CALIFORNIA COOL
PHOTO: MATT GEORGE

ROCHELLE BALLARD
NEW FEMININE ARCHETYPE
PHOTO: TOM SERVAIS

MATT KECHELE
BAHAMA BLUE
PHOTO: KEVIN WELSH

RUSTY KEAULANA
THREE-TIME WORLD
LONGBOARD CHAMP
PHOTO: CRAIG FINEMAN

DAVID EGGERS
IN SIMPLER TIMES
PHOTO: MIKE MOIR

The voracious world of surf stardom had its casualties. Matt Warshaw's look at the steep rise and fall of a young California hopeful served as a cautionary tale.

Volume 31 | *Number 2*

WHAT HAPPENED TO DAVID EGGERS?

BY MATT WARSHAW

Skip Mochetti, 37, is thick in the neck, chest and arms, completely fills out his navy blue three-piece suit, and has a 5-o'clock shadow that won't disappear under the sharpest razor. He's reserved but alert, with dark eyes taking everything in. This is a man of experience—it's obvious before he says a word. Mochetti teaches karate and has a bodyguard service, but today he's speaking as David Eggers' "business manager." He and Eggers drove up from La Jolla to South Orange County four hours earlier in Mochetti's dented, copper-colored, mid-'70s Thunderbird for a photo shoot/interview—Eggers' reintroduction to the surfing public after two and a half years of silence.

As Mochetti talks about his past, his easygoing tone of voice strikes a macabre chord, given the blunt impact of his words. Some hardships since the mid-'60s: four tours of duty in Vietnam, 16 bullet wounds across his upper body and arms, a POW for nine months, a broken neck from a 1987 car accident, half a cancerous lung removed in '88, an ongoing fight with lymphatic cancer, for which he takes morphine every six hours, and a recently diagnosed brain tumor.

Eggers, sitting on the opposite end of the couch from Mochetti, pushes his long blond hair away from his face, then makes an obvious point in a quiet voice: "And people think I've been through something, you know?"

The drinking and drugs came first, almost as soon as the contracts were signed, followed by what Eggers perceives as an effective campaign by teammates and fellow competitors to pressure him out of the game. Eggers puts it this way: "My surfing was there. Maybe the mental ability wasn't. For sure, I wasn't mature enough."

It's a heavy trial for the rare 16-year-old who comes along with the ability to shift the dynamics of the sport single-handedly. Once he's recognized, the surfing world—usually the only world that exists for the neophyte hero—will give everything, and expect the same in return. This is where a young surfer's life is not so much touched as altered—sometimes radically. It's impossible to say what route certain surfers would have taken had they not been dipped in gold mid-adolescence, but it's a fair bet every one of the great teen idols from the past 25 years—Lynch, Horan, Frohoff, Curren, Occhilupo, Potter, Archbold, Wood and Slater, for example—ricocheted at some point onto darker paths, previously unseen.

With David Eggers, again, it's impossible to say how big a hand fame had in changing his life. On first thought, he shrugs it off: "No, I probably would have done what I did regardless. Where I live, and what goes on in my town . . . hey, really, Southern California is not a great place to bring up children. You've got to keep your eye on 'em, always. I'm not the first kid to go down."

Later, though, he reverses field: "I jumped on the tour, started meeting people, mainly at parties—which I hardly ever used to go to—and all of a sudden, I don't know . . . things started to happen. I had the money; I had the fame; I had the attitude. Now, here was this whole new way of living. I mean, girls, parties, drinking, drugs . . . shit, I was 16, man, and could pretty much do whatever I wanted. Just show up somewhere and surf—that's all I had to do. Then go home, call my friends; they'd have some girls; I'd get a limo, and we were off."

Derek Hynd provided a one-man Greek chorus to the opera that was Australian Nicky Wood's pro career.

Volume 31 | Number 3

THE PHANTOM

BY DEREK HYND

It's 3:40 on a Saturday afternoon in Zarauz, Spain. Nicky Wood has just emerged from the shower and is playing the kid in the kitchen, hunting hidden chocolate in the icebox. His girlfriend, Natalie, the Black Widow, is in the smoke-hazed next room swapping caustic tales with driest hate-man, Gary Green. They're laughing. Wedged in the door frame is the rather large and timeless portrait king, Art Brewer, with camera-devouring subject, devouring the hard-brown-sugar rush, saying to me all the while how "the guy rips," and how "I'd never seen him, but I'd heard a lot. I just took 78 shots of his heat."

Wood's the same as always: quiet and unassuming, despite having posted the second-highest score of the year—99 points against Matt Hoy. He knows he's knocked the top off any critics but, more importantly, he thinks he's hit the judges with imagery solid enough to hold his name strong through the final stretch of the tour.

He moves into the bedroom to get some dirty water out of his ear and read his coaching report. Brewer is in there with him. It's a bizarre scene: huge man and spindly man. Nicky doesn't really know anything about Big Art—how, through the years, he's been tight with a lot of legends and has the full gamut of portraits stashed—but he warms to the chattering giant. Brewer, meanwhile, knows the keys of rare men and has Wood nailed as a "special one": different, with the Presence...the Destiny. At the moment, he's framing Nicky Wood like a fat cellar master storing fine wine.

Some see Nicky Wood as a latter-day Michael Peterson. He's called the Phantom on tour because, like M.P. in the '70s, he appears from nowhere at the last moment to grab his singlet, surf his heat, then vanish without a trace. It's become a game among the boys to spot the Phantom before his heat, but it's a game rarely won.

I walked down the beach at Zarauz with Matt Hoy before his heat against Wood. Nicky was nowhere in sight—and with paddle-out time already started. Also from Merewether, Australia, Hoy knew his opponent bloody well. "Where is he?" Hoy almost shouted, unsettled and wanting to target the Phantom. "He's a total idiot, isn't he?" Hoy lost the heat right there, blown out as he finally spotted Wood already halfway outside, way down the beach.

NICKY WOOD (LEFT) AND DEREK HYND
PHOTO: ART BREWER

The 1990 Eddie Aikau contest, held at Waimea Bay in Hawaii, was called the greatest single day of big-wave surfing ever seen. Brock Little's breathless drop was one of the reasons why.

Volume 31 | Number 5

PRESSURE DROP

BY BROCK LITTLE

I was in the second heat, along with Johnny Boy Gomes, Aaron Napolean, Richard Schmidt, Brian Keaulana, Dane Kealoha, Ken Bradshaw and four other guys. At the beginning of the heat, a 25-foot-plus closeout set came in. The trick to catching one of these kinds of waves at Waimea (not a top-to-bottom closeout but a rideable closeout) is to stay on the reef when the wave jacks. If you go too far out, the water's too deep, and it's impossible to get in.

As the set moved forward, the pack began stroking outside. I stayed farthest in, hoping to stay on the reef. When the set came, I realized I was still too far out—and I was 10 yards inside of anyone else. I paddled hard to get back to the lineup but didn't get there in time. Shit. One of the only closeout sets of the day, and I missed it.

Luckily, about 10 minutes later, another one came in. This time I stayed inside with Bradshaw and Aaron, and I was in perfect position for the first wave. It was huge . . . who knows, maybe 25 feet. I stroked into it, stood, looked down and swore. I knew I was in trouble—too much face, too many chops. It was possibly the biggest wave of my life. I got about halfway down, then couldn't stay on any longer. I didn't penetrate when I fell, I skipped. When I finally sank into the wave, I knew I'd go over the falls. Luckily, I grabbed a breath as I was on the way over. With that breath, I had enough oxygen to get through a fairly severe thrashing. That was a $55,000 wave, and I blew it.

BROCK LITTLE
AND THE LATE, GREAT EDDIE DROP AT WAIMEA
PHOTOS: ERIK AEDER

DARRICK DOERNER
SUPREME EXTREME AT PEAHI
PHOTO: DARRELL WONG

Sportswriter Bruce Jenkins profiled Darrick Doerner, a throwback to big-wave legends of old.

Volume 31 | *Number 9*

WATERMAN

BY BRUCE JENKINS

Pop Aikau passed away in late October 1989. He had withstood the pain of untold tragedy—the death of one son, then another, and the passing of his beloved wife. Finally, his own life gave out. Darrick Doerner had seen Pop just a few days before the end and remembers him saying, "Big surf coming. Two, weeks from now."

On Nov. 2, right on cue, it happened.

Pop was to be buried in Honolulu that day, and Doerner was prepared: he had a specially made lei of flowers from the rich maile vine to present as an offering from the Hui O He'e Nalu. But around 2 that morning, he was awakened by the sound of pounding surf outside his house at Backyards. As he stepped out for a firsthand look, Doerner saw nothing but white water—and he knew: it would be Waimea at dawn.

Now, you won't find too many people surfing 30-foot Waimea Bay before the sun comes up. The place is just too formidable; it requires thought and study. Nobody in his right mind would charge out there on dawn patrol like an excited freshman running down to Third Point Malibu. But Doerner knows the bay as few have: Every time it gets big, he's up in the middle of the night and can't get back to sleep—and he's the first one out the next morning.

"I was amping," he recalls. "Around 4 a.m., I got in my car and drove down there. I'd called Mark Foo the night before because I knew it was coming up and told him to be ready. I dropped over to his place around 5:30 and honked my horn . . . made all kinds of noise: 'Foo-Dog!' Nothing. No lights. So I drove back, parked up on the hill and waited."

With a dozen leis around his neck, Doerner watched a 30-foot closeout set greet the morning's first light. He checked his watch. Just 10 minutes later, another closeout set arrived, breaking completely across the bay. White water was pushing up past the beach, into the river and onto the grass—and, as Eddie Aikau always said, you don't surf Waimea under those conditions. Nevertheless, minutes later, Doerner was walking toward the point ready to go out.

"I was blind," he says. "Either I pulled it off, or I got slaughtered."

With absolutely no evidence the place was rideable, Doerner waited 20 minutes for a lull and hit the water, flowers still draped around him: "I didn't fool around; I headed straight out the middle. And I remember the incredible quiet as I paddled out during that lull. This was what I'd spent most of my life preparing for—all that training, all the paddling,

running on the beach—all for that day."

Up on the hillside, he spotted his friend Michael Ho, making a gesture that said, "No way." A few other cars had arrived. It was around 6:40, and Doerner was heading toward the lineup, alone. "My heart was just pounding, and the flowers were starting to slow me down. All of a sudden, I heard five or six horns going off. They could see a set coming on the horizon. I paddled over a solid 30-foot wave, then two more, just scratching to get over. Then it was quiet again."

Breathing a little easier, Doerner worked his way over to the takeoff zone. He saw a gigantic turtle, "Big as my car." He saw the moon in one direction, the rising sun in another. He cast aside the flowers, which looked gorgeous in the fresh, new light. The ritual, spontaneous and appropriate, was finished.

"I rode a dozen big waves with nobody out. No one around. It was the peak of my life, without a doubt. I wound up surfing the whole day—30 waves, 40, maybe even 50, at 20 to 25 feet. I lost count. About a week later, Clyde came down, and I told him the story about Pop predicting the swell, about the flowers, everything. He had to sit down. He started crying . . . chicken skin just popping out on his body. I had it, too. I still do."

SURFER asked the question—and was surprised by the answers from this disparate group of surfer/artists.

Volume 31 | *Number 11*

A QUESTION OF STYLE

JODIE COOPER
PROFESSIONAL SURFER
My car is a '62 Valiant—it looks like a small-version Batmobile. So I think my car has style. In general, though, it's all about being comfortable and secure with yourself. Also, I think to be stylish, you have to have some sense of arrogance.

LISA ANDERSEN
TRANSCENDING STEREOTYPES ONE HOT MOVE AT A TIME
PHOTO: TOM DUGAN

LISA ANDERSEN
PROFESSIONAL SURFER
Style is getting up in the morning, having a cup of joe and checking the waves. It's breaking in a pair of Levi's, getting them faded and full of stringy holes until they're just perfect.

CHRIS ISAAK
SINGER/SONGWRITER
Chet Baker had style. I did a session with him once. It was winter and real cold, and he came in wearing sandals, which was one of the coolest things I've ever seen. I told him I thought it would be great if he would do "Over the Rainbow," which, when you listen to it, is a very dark song. He looked at me and sneered, "I should probably do a Deep Purple song, too."

JOHN MILIUS
FILM DIRECTOR/WRITER/PRODUCER

Alexander the Great was seizing a fortress in India. He was leading a scalding assault when all others were swept from the ladder below him. He topped the wall, cleared the nearby opposition with his sword and suddenly found himself alone—gleaming in armor, obvious to everyone as Alexander the Great. Arrows clattered off his shield. He looked over his shoulder at his army, then turned toward the enemy city. He jumped forward. That's style.

CLOCKWISE FROM TOP: **KELLY SLATER**
UNBEATABLE FORM AT PIPELINE
PHOTO: JOHN BILDERBACK

GROMS
STYLE IS THE KID HIMSELF
PHOTO: JEFF DIVINE

JOHNNY BOY GOMES
WESTSIDE POWER
PHOTO: JOHN BILDERBACK

CHRISTIAN FLETCHER
SPINNING OUT IN CABO
PHOTOS: TOM SERVAIS

Surfing's gritty response to the '80s glam was crystallized in this short cultural study by Matt George.

Volume 33 | Number 1

FULL METAL RACKET

BY MATT GEORGE

She didn't actually cringe until Christian Fletcher stepped on board. I think it was his Brahma-bull nose ring that did the trick. I was watching her out of the corner of my eye, this young newlywed sitting across the aisle from me. She in a sundress and perky straw hat, her husband in crisp vacation Bermudas. They were the only people on the flight who were not involved with Herbie Fletcher's Cabo Classic. The couple had fallen into an uncomfortable silence shortly after discovering that a boisterous, long-haired, bandannaed, ragtag crew had turned the plane into a party bus. Had she been counting, she would have seen 47 imaginative tattoos, most of the surfers having long since removed their shirts.

The flight had been delayed for an hour now in the sweltering heat of San Diego. Nobody knew what the holdup was. Nobody cared, either. Earlier, I had seen real fear in the newlyweds' eyes when free beer was passed out to calm the mob. Her fear was justified. Since then, there had been two food fights, three B.A.s and a belching contest.

Just when the rage reached its crescendo, an extraordinary announcement was made by a harried stewardess. It seems there were too many surfboards to fit into the cargo hold. Our only choice was to leave some things behind. What was it going to be, she asked, our luggage or our surfboards?

A stunned silence fell. But it lasted only a moment. Then Robert Mahar yelled from the back, "Screw the luggage, man. Surf naked!"

A cheer went up, and the party resumed.

I felt a tap at my elbow. It was the newlywed. She looked at me and asked in a sweet voice, "Is that what you people are? Surfers?"

I replied that, why, yes, we were.

"Oh, thank God," she said. "I thought you were a motorcycle gang."

TALES FROM THE TUBE
ART: RICK GRIFFIN

Rick Griffin, 1944–1991

Volume 33 | *Number 1*

WARRIOR'S WAKE

BY STEVE BARILOTTI / ART BY RICK GRIFFIN

There's a real danger in having all your gods listed in your Rolodex, especially in a cult as young as surfing. Most of the pantheon are still alive, which makes them damnably human, so . . . vulnerable. A living legend is still quite capable of being overweight, aged, petty, broke, bigoted, drunk—of using terrible grammar or passing gas in your fawning presence. Clay feet are an occupational hazard.

But my sole encounter with Rick Griffin, the eccentric genius behind Murphy and some of surfing's most provocative and enduring icons, did nothing to magnify or diminish the mystique that enveloped him. There was no time for the paint to chip. It was terse, uncomfortable and over in seconds.

He was a bona fide hero of mine. I actually first knew of Rick Griffin not from SURFER Magazine but from Zap Comix, those brilliantly carnal "head comics" of my confused puberty. But later, as a surfer, I marveled at his masterful poster art for *Pacific Vibrations* and the classic *Five Summer Stories*, lingering outside the Granada Theater on those cold nights in Santa Barbara. When I went to work for SURFER some 10 years later, I was proud to be associated with him, however tenuously, via the magazine. Here was one of our alumni who had made the big time, had crossed over into doing world-acclaimed poster art for legends like Jimi Hendrix and the Grateful Dead, yet still returned sporadically to the magazine to contribute some mind-altering surf art.

This day, however, Rick had returned not to visit the old campus but to retrieve the original artwork he'd done more than 20 years earlier. I recall a lank, piratelike man in black jeans, calf-length boots and a tight black T-shirt, storming out of the SURFER offices with some drawings under his arm. He walked past me in a grumbling huff, clearly and sincerely pissed off. Apparently, over the hazy decades, some of his strips from the '60s—Murphy, the Griffin-Stoner adventures and various spot drawings—had simply disappeared into the black archives.

Although I was keen to introduce myself, to tell him how much I dug "Tales from the Tube" (the all-time jam session of surf comics), I didn't feel it right to disturb his flow of righteous anger. More to the point, he was a pretty big guy, and in his current mood, I felt he might have let me—yet another waffling magazine minion—have it where I lived. I backed off under his stare. He got into a nondescript van and rumbled away.

As the poet at the memorial said: "It was a raging time to meet Rick Griffin's eyes."

SURFER associate editor Ben Marcus introduced the world to Maverick's, a previously secret break in Northern California that would soon become the most famous big wave in the world.

Volume 33 | Number 6

COLD SWEAT

BY BEN MARCUS

15 YEARS OF SOLITUDE

Maverick's has an aura like Edward Scissorhands' mansion: gray, gloomy, isolated, inherently evil. The reef is surrounded by deep water and lies naked to every nasty thing above and below the Pacific: Aleutian swells, northwest winds, southeast storms, frigid currents, aggro elephant seals and wilder things that snack on aggro elephant seals. The shoreline is craggy rocks backed by sheer cliffs. Paddle through the lefts, and you skirt a twisted, tripled-up bowl that makes brave men nauseous. Paddle through the rights, and you fight a current that sweeps through two big pinnacles, then turns out to sea across one of the worst navigational hazards on the California coast. Maverick's radiates danger. It takes a peculiar sort of person to surf the place, alone, year after year.

Dave Parmenter's Alaskan surfari account not only stoked SURFER readers but was included in Houghton Mifflin's 1993 anthology of America's best sportswriting.

Volume 34 | Number 1

ALASKA

BY DAVE PARMENTER

As our strategy gelled, there remained one final obstacle, Mr. Bear. First and foremost, Alaska is bear country. Bears, bear tracks, bear shit and bear lore absolutely pepper the countryside. Every point in Alaska is Charlie Bear's Point. Charlie Bear don't surf, but he can run 35 mph, swim like Mark Spitz and climb a tree faster than a scalded cat.

Even in the urban areas, according to a newspaper account, bears "ruined by their taste in garbage" hang out at dumps like Insta-Teller muggers.

In the coupon section of the local newspaper, sandwiched between the Renuzit fragrance jars and the Hostess Ho-Ho's, is a device known as a Bear Bell. For 59 cents (with coupon) you get a cube-shaped bell that affixes to your clothing, the idea being that, when tromping over hill and dale, or taking an old mattress to the dump, you'll clang and peal like a Salvation Army Santa, thus signaling to any marauding bear, "Hey, comin' through."

Surprising a bear in repose (or any pose for that matter) is a pretty one-sided affair, if you're a stickler for all that statistical stuff. Of course, the Bear Bell is the rock-bottom, low-end ticket in bear repellent. It's sensible and field-tested effective, and for about five bucks, you can bell yourself, the fam, the mailman, baby Herman, even Rover. But, dammit, it's also un-American. It's what Gandhi would have done to ward off bears.

Which is why you should do what 99.999 percent of Alaskans do: purchase a big ol' mofo firearm and cad it everywhere like a fifth limb. This is the preferred linchpin in the guerrilla war with bears in Alaska.

Not that you'll ever really need your "smoke-wagon." Chances are, you'll never encounter a bear that will interrupt his berry-slurping or wood-shitting to charge you. But at least you can lend a hand in what seems to be a statewide industry of reducing wind resistance on road signs and mailboxes.

Being Lower 48 greenhorns in Alaska, we were constantly teased. "Look out for them bears, boys," they'd warn us with a twinkle in their eyes. We'd explain that Bob, Josh and I were from the notorious Red Triangle in Central California, and that once a person reconciled the fear of a sudden, fatal attack by a white shark, well, "bearanoia" seemed almost laughable. One wildlife expert stretching hard for a great sound byte on a local news show called the grizzly bear a "terrestrial version of the great white shark." We howled at that. Bears declare their major well in advance, unlike the stealth-torpedo tactics of a white. It's not like a grizzly suddenly rockets upward from some ursine gopher hole and takes your leg in a splintered second.

JOSH MULCOY
*BETWEEN GLACIERS AND
GRIZZLIES, YAKUTAT, ALASKA*
PHOTO: BOB BARBOUR

Matt Warshaw's rather serious exposé on sexism was countered by a clever—and titillating—cover blurb that read, "The Bikini Issue."

Volume 34 | Number 2

SEXISM SUCKS

BY MATT WARSHAW

Consider the durability of the word chick. The Beats invented the expression about 40 years ago; it got a push from the counterculture, easily survived the early '70s feminism and now stands as arguably the English-speaking world's most popular slang word for girl or woman. In surfing, virtually no other description for female exists.

As demonstrated by reigning ASP men's world champion Damien Hardman, after watching a women's heat last year, usage is as follows: "That's the best I've ever seen a chick surf."

An article on sexism in surfing, therefore, might begin with a quick lesson in semantics:

Chick is derogatory, in the same category as hebe, nigger and faggot. The fact that a world champion can nonchalantly describe a peer as a "chick" in an interview, without recrimination, only hints at the length, breadth and depth of sexism in surfing. Surfing's gender morals, in a word, suck. Hardman is champ; ignorance is king.

CLOCKWISE FROM TOP LEFT:

MAUREEN DRUMMY
PHOTO: RON BRAZIL

FRIEDA ZAMBA
PHOTO: DON KING

LAYNE "GIDGET" BEACHLEY
PHOTO: JEFF DIVINE

SERENA BROOKE
PHOTO: TOM SERVAIS

KEALA KENNELLY
PHOTO: RON BRAZIL

LISA ANDERSEN AND FANS
PHOTO: KEVIN WELSH

The humble birth of "tow-in" power surfing.

Volume 34 | Number 12

THE NEXT REALM?

BY BRUCE JENKINS

Bill Sickler had the binoculars out one day last winter, checking a huge north swell from a hillside spot above Sunset Beach. He was watching Laird Hamilton carve out a slice of the future, and he couldn't believe his eyes.

It takes a lot to impress Sickler. He was Jeff Hakman's roommate in the mid-'70s, and he's one of maybe a half-dozen guys to consistently surf Waimea, Sunset and Pipeline at maximum size over the last 15 years. Bill's idea of a leisurely afternoon is to body-surf Pipe in wild, jagged conditions with nobody else in the water.

But this was a vision for Sickler, something entirely new. Hamilton was more than a mile out at sea with Darrick Doerner, Buzzy Kerbox, a Zodiac boat and a WaveRunner. They were towing each other into Hawaiian-style 15-foot waves, picking them up out-

side Backyards, S-turning their way across the unbroken face, then jamming at full speed as the wave began to crest. The rides were almost surreal, lasting a minute or more, all the way through the inside section at Sunset, and they defined a bold new direction in big-wave surfing.

"What Laird was doing just blew my mind," said Sickler. "He had built up so much speed; he was just flying at the point where you usually start your takeoff. He was getting around sections that were simply impossible to make. It was windsurfers' capabilities being executed on a surfboard—I found out he was riding a 7' 2" with foot straps. He was cranking bottom turns where he was leaning so far over, the only thing in the water was the tip of that inside fin. Just flying, all the way

into the channel. I talked to a couple other guys who saw it, and it was like, we shouldn't even be out there with that kind of surfing going on."

Which is exactly the point. When it comes to tow-in surfing, you can appreciate it, study it, fantasize about it. But you won't be out there. Not unless you can match the knowledge and ability of Hamilton, Doerner and Kerbox, who are risking their lives and equipment to find empty waves at spots you can't even see from the beach.

"If you want to try this," says Doerner, "you'd better be able to swim 5 miles, hold your breath for more than two minutes in churning water and ride the biggest waves of your life in open ocean. You kids: don't try this at home."

Dave Parmenter's sojourn along the coast of Africa's Namibian desert.

Volume 35 | *Number 1*

ALONE

BY DAVE PARMENTER

NAMIBIA'S DIAMOND COAST
SOLITARY TREASURE
PHOTO: LANCE SLABBERT

I was sitting out in the lineup alone at a perfect left point on Namibia's Skeleton Coast, popping kelp bulbs and daydreaming between sets. The sun was going down, and I was trying, with as much empathy as I could muster, to imagine what it must have been like to be suddenly flung onto these shores after some disaster at sea and to realize the utter hopelessness of it. I pondered the riddle of the "crouching skeleton," a man found buried alive very close to where I was surfing, hunched in a little womblike grave. Most of the books dealing with the shipwreck lore of the Skeleton Coast found it to be a mystery. They concluded he must have been buried in a sandstorm while taking shelter in a hole. Just another riddle among hundreds on this coast.

Then I saw the jackal. He was on a little rise at the top of the point 30 yards away, just sitting on his haunches staring at me. At first, I thought he was curious, with his pricked-up ears and comically serious stare. In our culture, generations removed from real wilderness, we anthropomorphize animals. Dogs "smile," lions wear crowns, and bears are cute, cuddly things that bounce on our laundry.

I didn't take me long to understand that the jackal was sizing me up as potential prey, scanning through the predator checklist for some sign that I might fit the profile: old, young, weak, sick . . . alone? Even though there was absolutely no danger, it gave me a shiver to be considered food, as well as a little insight into why a man might prefer premature burial to being jackal fodder like the countless torn seals that carpeted every square foot of shoreline for miles around the rookery at the cape.

Carnage is what the Skeleton Coast is all about. The name is derived from the profusion of bones strewn along a 400-mile swath on the northern coast of Namibia. From literally any random vantage point, some sort of pitiful remains can be seen: bleached whale ribs, broken-backed ships, piles of seal bones and, perhaps, the tangled skeleton of some hapless castaway who made it ashore and died wishing he hadn't.

I was pretty keen on making it to shore myself. The last set of the day hit the outer indicator at Robbenspunt and filed down the half-mile point toward my lineup, the second perfect left point in a two-mile stretch. With a rookery of 100,000 Cape fur seals just up the point, there's a pretty good chance of some sort of encounter with a white shark. Also, lions have been known, in years of drought, to sneak up on seals as they sleep and have a little high-cholesterol snack. Most surfers live in a smug cocoon of invulnerability, and why not? With a good car in view, a jerrican of water, a wetsuit, Swiss Army knife, duct tape and a little common sense, surfers are practically immortal. But with the sun all but gone, surfing alone without a leash, the nearest town 100 miles away, I began to feel the hair stand up on the back of my neck and shivered to some involuntary primordial warning surging down my spine. A quarter-mile down the point, Lance had lit the car up as he packed away the gear—a cozy sphere of warmth and safety. I was tired of littering in the food chain. The first wave of the set approached, a perfect 5-foot wall that roped down the point for 200 yards. I caught it, pulled my feet out of Triassic Park as I stood and glided toward the 20th century.

TOM CURREN
*FLUID ELOQUENCE IN
HINAKUS, INDONESIA*
PHOTO: TED GRAMBEAU

"Tom Curren Writes!" read the **SURFER** headline, and he did, with almost as much verve as his surfing on this never-before-seen Indonesian reef break.

Volume 35 | *Number 11*

WHO ARE THESE CHILDREN?

BY TOM CURREN

Equatorial flora and fauna, everything is growing. This is the spore of the world. Things unseen carry the Power of Creation and, in turn, are carried by wind and sea to a final destination where they thrive or die. Oddest of all is the festering envy that many village people display toward foreigners. Out here, where there is little tourist traffic, this phenomenon is nonexistent. Out here, the few locals we meet are more curious than anything. They simply want to know what we're about.

Travelers will save up for a vacation that will be spent under subhuman conditions and wonder how to manage not having to go back to the human race. Once you've given yourself over to a place like this, you can forget about Western ways. Our values are shown to be nihilistic and devoid of any use for past or future. We think we're living each moment to the fullest, when it's really just hollow entertainment. But we're very good at it, of course, all this slickly packaged stimulus. We make great cartoons.

Surfing's version of the caveman, meanwhile, has dropped from the world and landed here. He sets up camp and waits for months on end to stand in a cave for a 75-yard stretch. Malaria stories are commonplace. But even more deadly and widespread are reported cases of hopelessness when faced with returning to Sydney, Tokyo or L.A. Once home, they quickly rustle up enough quid to get back to these reef breaks. Also remarkable are the Euros who just keep on backpacking on some kind of never-ending Euro pass. They come to take up surfing with their brethren, lolling about in the lineup, oblivious to the potential danger of collision. Ah, paradise as it was and never will be again.

A shift in local values toward materialism is accelerated by the many surfers who visit this new world on their own terms with their own toys. Because if there's a group of people with more extravagant needs, I've yet to find them. How will the surfers who come through here remain in the minds of the villagers? Like tourists? Worse? In any case, these people will soon see plenty of us; they live too close to too much great surf. It will be an amazing microcosm; once the hotels and surf camps are established, the scene will wander out to the next place on the periphery. And then the boom will repeat.

SHAWN BRILEY
*THROWING HIS WEIGHT
AT INSIDE SUNSET*
PHOTO: JOHN BILDERBACK

**Self-destructive or just self-confident? North Shore hell-kid
Shawn Briley blurs the lines in this interview with Ben Marcus.**

Volume 35 | Number 12

THE ANGEL INSIDE

BY BEN MARCUS

HERE YOU ARE, ONLY 19 YEARS OLD . . .
Twenty.

*. . . ONLY 20 YEARS OLD, AND ALREADY THE WORLD IS FULL OF SHAWN
BRILEY STORIES. YOU'RE BECOMING THE FLIPPY HOFFMAN OF THE '90s.*
What are you talking about?

*IT SEEMS LIKE ANYONE WHO SPENDS MORE THAN 24 HOURS WITH
YOU COMES AWAY WITH SOME KIND OF NEAR-DEATH EXPERIENCE.*
Who said that?

*TODD CHESSER TALKED ABOUT THE TIME HE NEARLY DIED IN YOUR
JEEP AS IT SKIDDED OUT OF CONTROL AT 60 MPH INTO THE OPPOSITE
LANE WITH A CAR COMING AT YOU, NEAR THE WAIMEA BRIDGE.*
No comment.

*ANOTHER ONE OF YOUR FRIENDS DESCRIBED VERY VIVIDLY THE
SIGHT OF YOU SITTING IN THE FRONT SEAT OF YOUR CAR WITH A GUN
HELD TO YOUR HEAD, CALMLY TALKING SOME TOWN GANGSTER OUT
OF BLOWING YOUR BRAINS OUT.*
I don't want to talk about that.

*AN EARLY VERSION OF THE ENDLESS SUMMER II HAD A SHOT OF YOU
TAKING OFF ON A 6-FOOT WAVE IN THE WAIMEA SHOREBREAK AND*

GOING HEAD-FIRST OVER THE FALLS INTO 2 FEET OF WATER.
They cut that out of the movie? Shoots.

WHY WERE YOU SURFING THE SHOREBREAK AT WAIMEA BAY?
I didn't want to surf 12- to 15-foot Pinballs with a bunch of dummies. It was
winter. There wasn't anything else happening on the North Shore that was good
to surf. I'm radical, so I did something radical. It's fun, charging the shorebreak.

*WHY DO YOU DO THOSE THINGS? WHY DO YOU TAKE OFF ON CLOSE-
OUTS AT PIPE? WHY DO YOU COLOR YOUR HAIR GREEN? WHY DO YOU
DRIVE CRAZY? WHY DO YOU DO THINGS THAT COULD MAIM YOU FOR
LIFE?*
Why do I do things like that? You should know that. It was in SURFER
Magazine a couple issues ago.

WHICH ONE?
The one with the epic photo of Shawn Briley on the cover. I have it right here
in my hand. Look on page 70. It's a caption about me by none other than Kelly
Slater. He says, "There are people you'll watch surf and you'll say to yourself,
'God, that guy really loves the camera.' Shawn, I feel, is one of those guys. But
somewhere along the line, he learned to enjoy it and get really good at it." There
it is. I do crazy things because I love the camera and I love attention. Kelly
Slater said so.

PAT CURREN
PHOTO: ART BREWER

A reverential portrait of '50s legend Pat Curren and the often strained relationship with his brilliant son Tom.

Volume 36 | Number 3

FATHER, SON, HOLY SPIRIT

BY BRUCE JENKINS

A look into the Curren family would not be complete without the perspective of Sam George: "Tommy told me one time that his dad disapproved of what he does, being a pro and competitive surfer. It hadn't been spoken in words, but Tommy got the feeling his dad wasn't real stoked about the direction he went in surfing. Now that's a pretty tough thing to live with. You become the greatest surfer ever, and your dad, who was also a great surfer, doesn't approve of it? The last time Tom saw him, I think they reached some kind of resolution."

A Curren story was relayed to Sam George: Apparently, a year or two ago, someone sent Pat a surf video that showed Tommy, in full glory, ripping waves all over the world. Pat was reportedly so overwhelmed by the scope of his son's work, his eyes teared up.

"I don't know if that really happened," George said. "But I hope it did."

Mark Foo, 1958-1994.

Volume 36 | Number 5

THE FINAL CHARGE

BY MATT WARSHAW

Mark Foo died surfing Maverick's on Friday, Dec. 23, 1994, and that's as fixed and settled as it gets. Almost everything else about the day, almost every line of thought, remains in a state of flux and conjecture.

How did Foo die? Drowning followed by head wound or the other way around? Why did Foo die? Random occurrence or destiny? Did it have to do with all the cameras on the scene? Lack of sleep? Not knowing the lineup and taking off too far back? Was his board too long? Did he rush into it without looking the place over carefully? Was he out of practice?

How is it that Foo fell off at the peak, in the middle of the action, with a dozen experienced big-wave surfers outside (including Brock Little, Mike Parsons, Ken Bradshaw, Mark Renneker, Evan Slater and Jeff Clark), three boats in the channel, more than a hundred spectators and photographers watching from land, and a helicopter circling overhead, and nobody saw him surface and drift away to the south?

"Everyone wants answers and wants 'em fast," Bradshaw said a week after Foo died. "In general, I think Mark's death was a fluke. But people's thinking on the whole thing is still evolving. Mine is for sure. I'm still thinking about it all the time."

MARK FOO
"TO ME, IT'S NOT TRAGIC DYING DOING SOMETHING YOU LOVE"
PHOTO: ROB GILLEY

Serving to counteract the shock of Mark Foo's death at Maverick's, this single glorious ride by a 16-year-old surfer from Santa Cruz reaffirmed the life of the big-wave surfer.

Volume 36 | Number 5

CINDERELLA VS. GODZILLA

BY MATT WARSHAW

It's a Cinderella story. Or, perhaps, a Cinderella-meets-Godzilla story. On Sunday night, Dec. 18, 16-year-old Santa Cruz surfer Jay Moriarity is on duty at Pleasure Point Pizza. He rolls some dough; he slices some pepperoni; he makes a big batch of sauce. Bored, he dials the National Weather Service hot line and hears a reading off the Point Arena buoy that's bigger than anything he's ever heard. Genuinely amped at the thought of riding 20-foot surf the next day, Jay goes surfing by himself in the moonlight that night in 10-foot faces at Pleasure Point. He is home by midnight and up at 4:30 the next morning. He loads two 10-foot-plus guns into his mom's Datsun truck and drives north.

At Pillar Point Harbor, Jay snags a boat ride with photographer Bob Barbour. The boat stops in the channel around 7 a.m., and they get a look at the conditions. Maverick's is humongous. The biggest waves Jay has ever seen are bowling onto the reef, held up until the last minute by a 5.9 high tide and 20-knot offshores. The water is in the low 50s, the air even colder. There are 10 guys out, including Evan Slater, Darryl Virostko, the Wormhoudt brothers, Alistair Kraft, Nacho Lopes and Chris Brown. Jay watches from the boat for 20 minutes. The sets are consistent, but few are being ridden. It is too big, too windy and too high tide. Evan Slater paddles for a set, sideslips down the face and bounces 3 feet in the air before going over the falls.

Jay paddles out soon after, passing people frozen by the weather or nerves or both. He finds his lineup at the top of the bowl and waits no more than 10 minutes for a set to come through. He paddles for a set, gets to his feet and is launched into big-wave history.

ARE YOU OUT OF YOUR MIND?
I thought I had it. To me, it looked good. But it turned out to be a nightmare.

WHAT WENT WRONG?
I was a little too deep, but I feel like if the wind wasn't on it, I could have made it. Everything looked good as I was paddling for it, and as I started to stand up, I thought, "This will be a cool wave. It'll be fine." I got to my feet, and for a split second it felt OK. Then the whole wave ledged out, and I could feel myself getting lifted by the wind. The wave went straight up, and I had a moment to look down into a bottomless ocean. I had time to think, "Oh, shit. This is not good." The next thing I knew, I was getting drilled.

HOW DID YOU HANDLE IT?
From what I've learned about wiping out, you just have to relax and let it beat the crap out of you and hope you come up. So I relaxed.

DID IT HURT?
Yeah, it hurt. The impact felt like I was getting hit by 10 semi-trucks all at once. I was amazed by how hard it hit me, and I was amazed that it didn't rip me to pieces.

I'VE SEEN THE VIDEO OF THAT WAVE. FROM THE TIME YOU FALL INTO THE LIP UNTIL THE TIME YOUR HEAD POPS UP IN THE WHITE WATER IT TOOK 21 SECONDS.

It felt like I was down there for years. The impact pushed me so deep I actually hit the bottom on my back. I was thinking, "Wow, I've never heard of anyone hitting bottom out here. I hope I come up." I somehow got my feet under me and pushed off. It seemed like it took me forever to get to the surface. I was stroking up and up with my eyes open, but it was completely black. It was black forever. Then I could see a little light and I popped up.

DID YOU GET CLOSE TO PANICKING?
When I was under, I was thinking, "If I don't get to the surface soon, I'll get hit by the second one for sure." But I was calm. I was scared, but I wasn't going to panic. I came up a little dazed but not gasping. The second wave tumbled me around a little bit, but it was nothing compared to the first one. I popped up after the second wave and saw Evan in the lineup. He had caught the wave after mine and was waiting in the channel to see if I was OK.

WERE YOU?
I was seeing stars, and I think I was dazed a bit, but I was OK. Evan stuck around to make sure I could make it by myself. My leash was still attached to my leg, and I had about 2 feet of surfboard attached to my leash. I found the other half of the board and paddled over to the boat. Bob, his friend Kyle and the boat driver all asked if I was OK. I got in the boat, took my other 10' 8" out of the bag and waxed it up. Then I paddled back out.

YOU'RE GNARLY.
I don't know. I was OK. As I was paddling back into the lineup, I saw Anthony Ruffo, and he said, "You're heavy, man." When I got to the lineup, Josh Loya and some other guys said, "That was heavy." I sat out at the peak for about 45 minutes before I caught another wave. It was a set and I made it, and from then on I was fine. I surfed for five more hours and caught eight waves.

JAY MORIARITY
AND HIS EPIC MAVERICK'S ENCOUNTER
PHOTO: BOB BARBOUR

With American surfers dominating virtually every professional division, Sam George spoofed the chest-thumping of John Witzig's "We're Tops Now," written 28 years before.

Volume 36 | Number 6

WHO'S TOPS NOW?

BY SAM GEORGE

Perhaps the blame belongs to their surf mags, all three of which have reduced themselves from sources of national pride to cleverly packaged smut, pandering to the masturbatory fantasies of adolescent males. (A recent issue of *Australian Surfing Life* included more than 15 references to sex and sex organs, including an editorial on penis enlargement and a cartoon of Martin Potter go-go dancing in a G-string. And *Tracks* ran an article on Kelly Slater that included a full-frontal nude portrait of Pamela Anderson.) If the Aussie mag's vision of a country obsessed with autoerotica is accurate, that could explain much: the next generation of hot young surfers must be exhausted from spending all that time in the "loo."

World Champion Lisa Andersen almost single-handedly changed the perception of women's surfing in the '90s with a potent contrast of both invincibilty and vulnerability.

Volume 37 | Number 2

LISA ANDERSEN

BY BEN MARCUS

The telephone rings again. A woman with the remnants of a New York accent asks for Lisa.

"I'm going to look for her right now. Who is this?"

"This is her mother."

It's Lorraine. I introduce myself as the guy who's going to tell Lisa's story and ask if I can pry a little.

"A little is OK."

"What do you think of your daughter?"

"I think she's terrific. She set out to accomplish something and put her mind to it, and she did it. Most young people today don't."

"Was she always so terrific?"

"Maybe she was and I didn't know it. When Lisa started surfing here in Florida, I didn't know much about it, and I thought it was a bad scene. I didn't want her in it."

"How much trouble was she?"

"She was pretty terrible. She couldn't wait to grow up and was always hanging around with the older kids. My rules were: in bed by 9 p.m. and no later than 10. One night, I went in there and she was gone. She had snuck out the window and met a girl-friend and they were with some older boys."

"Maybe they were just fixing dings or something."

"I don't know about that."

"Where does Lisa get her athletic ability?"

"Maybe from me. I was a tomboy like her, and I was a dancer for 15 years."

"Lisa is pretty graceful. Are you graceful?"

"I suppose I was. I'd like to think so."

"Are you stubborn and single-minded?"

"I think she gets that from her father."

"What was he like?"

"Do we have to talk about him?"

"No. Why did Lisa run away from home?"

"You're not going to talk about that runaway stuff, are you? It's been done over and over, and we're tired of reading about it."

"It's hard to tell her story without it."

"Oh, well, when she ran away from home, and I didn't know where she was, that was a scare."

"How old was Lisa?"

"Sixteen. She left just after her sophomore year of high school. I went on vacation, and she stayed home. When I got back, she was gone. I found a note in her room saying she was going to be the number-one surfer in the world."

"Did you know where she went?"

"I had no idea. She was gone for a year, and I didn't hear a thing."

"A year? That's a heavy deal to pull on your mom."

"She really wanted to go surfing, I guess."

"How did you find her?"

"I found her through a jaywalking citation that came in the mail. She was in Huntington Beach, and I did some tracking and found where she was staying. I left a message saying that her mom called and that she could call back whenever she wanted."

"She called?"

"Yes, she did, and she started sending press clippings showing her results as a surfer. That whole thing brought us closer together, and we've been like two peas in a pod ever since."

LISA ANDERSEN
ALL ON HER OWN
PHOTOS: TOM SERVAIS

TOM CARROLL
DEEP IN ENEMY TERRITORY
PHOTO: TOM SERVAIS

Localism, that territorial vestige of the 1970s, still found a home in Central California.

Volume 37 | Number 8

FOREIGN SPECIES

BY STEVE BARILOTTI

Welcome to California, Tom Carroll. Now go home.

Like any unruly drunken uncle at Thanksgiving who spies a mixed-race couple at the table and decides to make a scene, a small crew of locals at Diablos made it absolutely clear that our presence at their surf break was, if not unwelcome, at least totally unexpected. It's odd, because the aggression seemed unnecessary. There were never more than 10 guys out, sparsely scattered over two separate takeoff zones. And our photographers were nowhere in sight.

It was a beautiful slack-wind day, and Diablos was throwing out an endless train of fat, sucky double-overhead ledges. A wealth of waves. But that didn't seem to be the point.

Once they paddled out, the surf stars' appearance in the lineup created a schism among the Diablos aboriginals, putting them in a quandary as to whether to be ritually fierce and territorial or stoked that a pair of international surf legends were sharing—no, make that ripping—their home break. The locals certainly had the gumpy thing down pat: monkish black wetsuits, stink-eye stares, muttered threats and blatant snakes. There was one older male who insisted on screaming obscenities at anyone who randomly strayed within a 20-foot killing radius. When he saw one of his tribe talking to Banks, he went ballistic: "Whattaya doing, Chipper? This ain't no f---in' whorehouse!"

Steve Hawk's fictional humor piece was in fact a prescient vision of 21ST-century world surf travel.

Volume 37 | Number 10

TRESTLES COMES TO SUMBA

BY STEVE HAWK

JUNE 22, 2033

My cover is blown early. Three days after we set sail from Darwin, the skipper of the S.S. *Morning Light*, the curiously named Capt. Blaine Lane, pays a visit to my first-class cabin. He is pleasant enough: cordial, humble, yet clearly a man of authority. And maybe the best-groomed surfer I've ever met.

Unfortunately, I'd hoped to spend my two weeks aboard the *Morning Light* anonymously. I wanted the crew and my fellow passengers to think I was just another paying schlub hoping to score a few choice Indo barrels. But now that they know I'm writing a story about the trip, the Heisenberg principle will be in effect: Everything they do will be tainted by the fact that they're worried about how they'll look in print. Nobody will act naturally.

Usually I don't mind if people know my role. After 20 years as SURFER's online travel editor, I've learned that it works to my advantage to whip out press credentials now and then. How do you think we discovered Lenin's Tomb, that mile-long sandspit left in Kamchatka [see "Seaside Comes to Siberia," Vol. 51, No. 3] back in 2010? That never would have happened if the mayor of Petropavlovsk, hungry for some press, hadn't given us free use of a military helicopter for a week. Same with Big Mac's, the now-famous open-ocean peak we found five years later down near McDonald Island [see "Maverick's Comes to Antarctics," Vol. 56, No. 7]. Hell, that one was all but financed by the Australian Board of Tourism.

But this time, aboard the *Morning Light*, my intention was to sit quietly in the corners and mock. How could I resist? When I found out that Circus-Circus Cruise Lines had actually transformed one of its smaller ships into a surfers-only luxury liner, I booked a berth on the maiden voyage with a smirk on my face. It promised to be a gonzo mother lode: 200 lazy, fat-cat surfers and their families being led around Indonesia by their dainty wrists.

Roulette at night, shuffleboard in the morning, sick reef-pass pits in the afternoon. I planned to portray them as the lazy fools they are.

My outrage grew when Circus-Circus revealed that the Indonesian government had granted the cruise line exclusive surfing access to the entire island of Sumba. (Imagine the size of *that* bribe.) The theory was obvious: you need a lot of empty breaks if you're going to drop anchor with a couple of hundred kooks on board.

I've had some magical sessions on those very reefs back when they were open to the world, so it is with mixed feelings that I accept Capt. Lane's invitation to dinner.

"It's an honor to meet the famous Kevin Peterson," the captain says as we wait for our faux filets. "I've been reading your stories since I was a grom. In fact, it was your article on that river mouth in Karachi ["Pipeline Comes to Pakistan," Vol. 45, No. 8] that convinced me to quit school and travel."

I smile but can't quite hide a wince. I've heard similar pronouncements before and they always inflict pain. Glancing around the room, which appears to be filled with middle-aged spread sheeters and their genetically enhanced wives, I feel even deeper dread. How many of these surfers are here because of the surf media's relentless pursuit of exotic new surf spots? How many are here because of *me*?

As I fight off a wave of self-doubt, one of Capt. Lane's tuxedo-clad underlings rushes to the table in a barely controlled panic. He leans over and whispers something in the captain's ear. The captain's eyes widen, and he stands abruptly.

"You'll have to excuse me," he says. "I'm sure it's nothing to be alarmed about, but it would appear that we're under attack."

ICELAND
*LIVED UP TO ITS NAME
ON THIS CHILLY—AND
REMARKABLE—SURFARI*
PHOTO: JEFF DIVINE

The search for surf continued, sometimes to the end of the Earth—or at least the ice pack.

Volume 38 | Number 3

ICELAND

BY DAN DUANE

PART ONE: BLAA LONID

In the end, we had the experience surfers all dream of. But on our third day in Iceland, as the seven of us glumly ate a standard local breakfast of coffee, toast and pickled herring, nothing seemed less likely. I don't know about you, but I'm not crazy about pickled herring before noon. Or at any time, really. Picking at my food and watching storm clouds whip drizzle across the windows, I got so depressed I tried to think instead of Olof, the lovely local girl refilling the coffee pot. She had a sweet grace about her and the flawless skin all the natives did. I clearly wasn't going to get the Arctic tube vision I'd been craving—the one that would save me from my awful fate as a hopeless tube barney—but maybe I'd bring home something a little warmer, a little longer-lasting: it wasn't at all hard to see flying Olof out to California for a few weeks of fun. You see, months before, when I'd called the Iceland Tourist Board, a man named Einar Gustavsson had said, "Surfing? In Iceland? It's never been done, but why not? We are even blond!" Old Einar had then Fed-Exed me a travel video called *Iceland: The Hot Spot* (It just may melt your heart), full of crystal blue skies, beaches with offshore winds. Waves? "As big as houses!" Einar had assured me. "You won't believe it!" And, to clinch the deal, he'd told me all about Iceland's legendary women, including two Miss Worlds in the past 10 years. And that morning in the hotel, it was looking like the women were the only part of his pitch that hadn't been an outright hoax. I just needed to think of an opening gambit.

We'd spent those first few days searching a coastline so surreal in its austerity—so blackened and mystical—that all comparisons failed. Bubbled, broken lava lay hardened beneath spent cinder cones; low clouds swirled and blew over distant mountains, and, in the relentless rain, little stone cairns marked the mones of fairies, not to be disturbed. In the lead car: intrepid "Surf Docs" Mark Renneker and Kevin Star, for whom genuine surf exploration was an abiding passion, as well as Mark's morbidly funny painter girlfriend, Jessica Dunne. And in our car, trailing them like wayward FBI agents still suspicious of long-hairs: Wingnut™, fresh in from a Robert August event in Japan; Jeff Divine, patiently biding his time; Donovan Frankenreiter, obsessing on the foot-thick down comforters and polar bear rugs he was certain the local girls all had; and me, giving up yet again on getting piped and plotting instead my move on Olof (especially in view of a recent study showing that 70 percent of all Icelandic children are born out of wedlock). In the perpetual Arctic twilight, we'd driven miles of jeep track beneath 10-story NATO radar dishes that still gave directions to a forgotten Armageddon, peered in the shuttered windows of fortresslike houses and watched the surf do what it does the world over in 30-knot onshores: suck. At nearly every beach, the detritus of recent shipwrecks lay scattered among the rocks, including that of a trawler battered against a jetty by a recent storm. A rescue 'copter had been unable to help, we were told, and the families had watched from T.V. as all hands were lost. Every Icelander we told

of our desire to surf said exactly the same thing: "You will die."

So now, in a warm and bright room typical of this nation that rarely goes outdoors, with a view of a hot blue lake in black lava flow (fed by effluent from a geothermal power plant), I prepared to move in. Doc was absorbed in expertly picking our next destination. (Doc loves nothing more that the search, and in preparation for this trip into truly unexplored surf territory, he'd acquired old Defense Department amphibious landing maps for the entire Icelandic coastline and was receiving detailed daily weather faxes. We would have been utterly lost without him.) Meanwhile, Kevin, a truly world-class Alpine climber, was distracting Frankie and Divine with mountaineering horror stories. Seeing the window, I got to work, engaging Olof in teaching me to pronounce her name. I'd watch her lips as she said it very slowly, and then I'd repeat it, and then she'd laugh in my face. And then we'd start over. "Look," I told her, when the game got old, "we'll be in the capital tonight, meeting the owner of a snowboard show. Maybe you and I could have a drink . . ."

She blushed, glanced over to Frankie. "Well, uh, you see . . ."

The long-hair was singing the opening bars of "Giver Man," a tune by his band, Sunchild.

"I've arranged," she said apologetically, "to show your friend . . . with the hair . . . around the city." Then, as an afterthought—perhaps noticing my crestfallen expression—she added, "And you can come, too, if you want."

Todd Chesser, 1970–1997.

TOP: TODD'S SMILE
PHOTO: ART BREWER

BELOW: TODD CHESSER
PHOTO: JEFF DIVINE

Volume 38 | Number 7

NOT FADE AWAY

BY BEN MARCUS

Todd Chesser no longer prowls the Earth. It's impossible, but it's true. The same ocean that gave Todd Chesser his character—his courage, his pride, his love, his humor, his reason for living—came along and took that life away. Chesser knew the risks, took them, and now the risks have taken him. Fair fight but the wrong side won.

Out along Kaena Point, where, according to the Hawaiian myth, Chesser's spirit left this Earth, there is a golf cart without a driver, beautiful surfboards without a rider, a bed without him in it and a friend, Jessie Lovett, left wondering how he'll find another roommate like Todd Chesser. In that same house, there is a young woman, Janet Rollins, who is devastated by the loss of the man she was going to marry. "We were best friends. The way he made me feel was just extraordinary. No one has or ever will make me feel the way he did."

Todd Chesser no longer prowls the North Shore—the slide shows and parties, the corner tables at Café Haleiwa, the remote outer reefs or the inner recesses of Sunset Beach. Off the Wall will never be the same. A safer place for bodyboarders, perhaps, but a lesser place for Shane Dorian and Kelly Slater and all the guys who loved to hear Chesser's mad cackle ringing from deep inside the barrel. The outer reefs will never be the same. A kinder place for the tow-in guys on their Jet Skis but a lesser place for Keoni Watson and Chris Malloy and all the guys who loved to hear Chesser's mad cackle as he paddled for waves he shouldn't have paddled for.

The North Shore is a lonelier place, a quieter place, a lesser place without Todd Chesser. The wave that rolled over Chesser left hundreds of friends who will miss him terribly, hundreds of people who wish they'd hung out with him more, bought him breakfast, said good-bye.

Todd Chesser is gone—the love, the courage, the muscle, the pride, the humor. His strong body was turned to ashes and is now a part of the reef near Himalayas. His spirit remains. As the longing for Todd fades and the memories take over, what will remain is the first thing anybody noticed about Todd: the smile. Chesser's smile will hang over the North Shore forever, reminding everyone to have courage, have pride, take chances, have fun, be yourself, love your friends, be honest, go hard and smile.

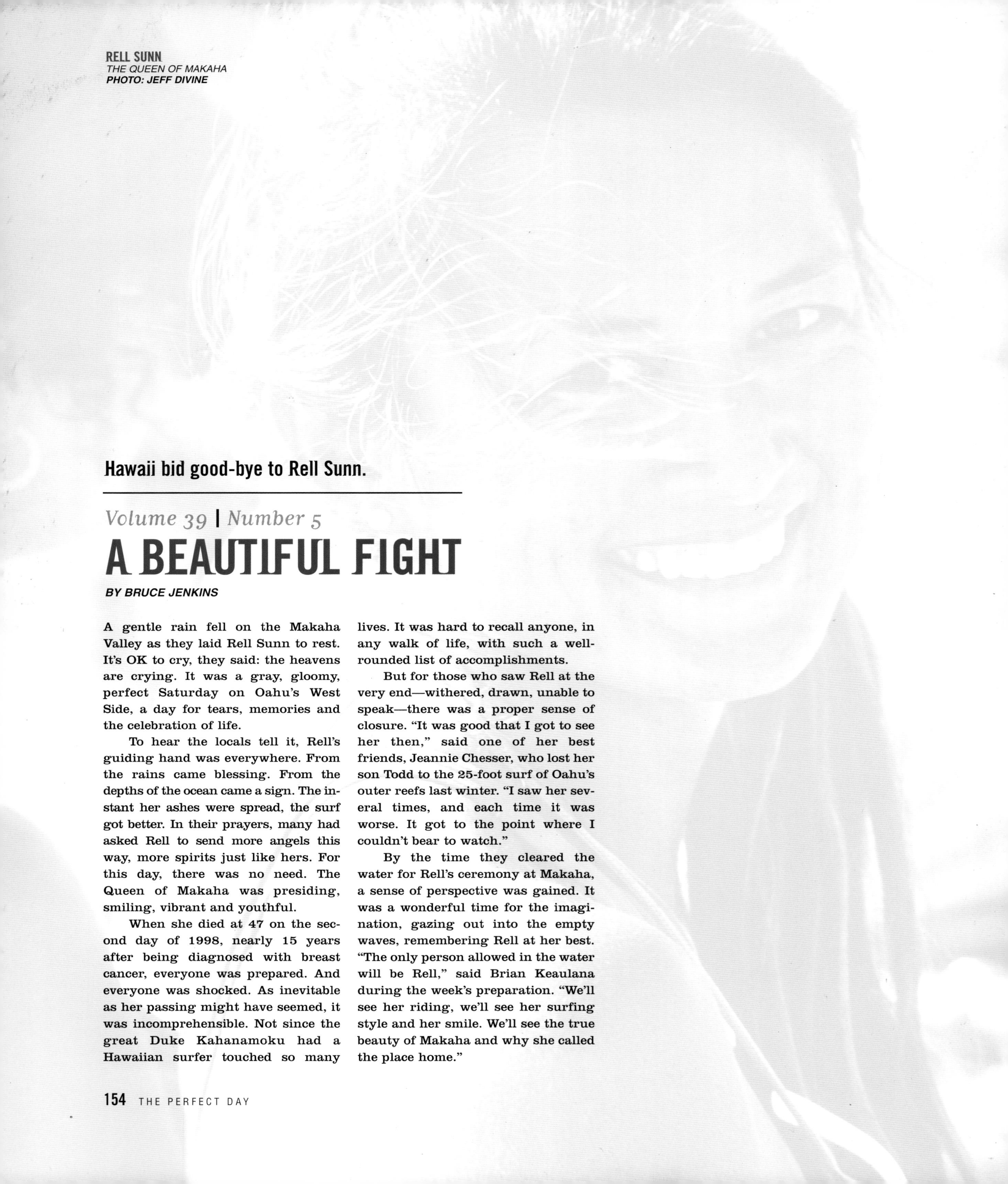

RELL SUNN
THE QUEEN OF MAKAHA
PHOTO: JEFF DIVINE

Hawaii bid good-bye to Rell Sunn.

Volume 39 | Number 5

A BEAUTIFUL FIGHT

BY BRUCE JENKINS

A gentle rain fell on the Makaha Valley as they laid Rell Sunn to rest. It's OK to cry, they said: the heavens are crying. It was a gray, gloomy, perfect Saturday on Oahu's West Side, a day for tears, memories and the celebration of life.

To hear the locals tell it, Rell's guiding hand was everywhere. From the rains came blessing. From the depths of the ocean came a sign. The instant her ashes were spread, the surf got better. In their prayers, many had asked Rell to send more angels this way, more spirits just like hers. For this day, there was no need. The Queen of Makaha was presiding, smiling, vibrant and youthful.

When she died at 47 on the second day of 1998, nearly 15 years after being diagnosed with breast cancer, everyone was prepared. And everyone was shocked. As inevitable as her passing might have seemed, it was incomprehensible. Not since the great Duke Kahanamoku had a Hawaiian surfer touched so many lives. It was hard to recall anyone, in any walk of life, with such a well-rounded list of accomplishments.

But for those who saw Rell at the very end—withered, drawn, unable to speak—there was a proper sense of closure. "It was good that I got to see her then," said one of her best friends, Jeannie Chesser, who lost her son Todd to the 25-foot surf of Oahu's outer reefs last winter. "I saw her several times, and each time it was worse. It got to the point where I couldn't bear to watch."

By the time they cleared the water for Rell's ceremony at Makaha, a sense of perspective was gained. It was a wonderful time for the imagination, gazing out into the empty waves, remembering Rell at her best. "The only person allowed in the water will be Rell," said Brian Keaulana during the week's preparation. "We'll see her riding, we'll see her surfing style and her smile. We'll see the true beauty of Makaha and why she called the place home."

JOEL TUDOR
WITH FEET FIRMLY IN BOTH ERAS
PHOTO: TOM SERVAIS

Is Tudor the best modern longboarder or simply the best ever?

Volume 39 | *Number 10*

JOEL TUDOR JUST WANTS TO TURN YOU ON

BY STEVE BARILOTTI

Bird's horn breathes a violet rainbow through Old Blue, fills the empty space between us, indigo. It swirls up and is sucked out the wind wing, tatters and scatters over the little gray waves like a million musical jacaranda blossoms.

And Tudor is behind the wheel of Old Blue—his beat 1964 Chevy Bel Air with rusty Bay Standard racks—one eye on the road, the other on the little waves as we ascend from Torrey Pines State Beach into the billion-dollar biotech ghetto overlooking Black's. The latest El Niño storm has moved in, clocking the wind sideshore. He peels off an orange slice and the air fills with sweet citrus perfume layered over a bass note of strong red hair. He offers it across the bench seat: "You want some of this, Chief?"

"Chief" is Joel's all-purpose nickname for anybody he's not sure of. Friendly, but with a touch of locker-room insolence. He's been dealing with adults his whole life and has found little to impress him. Raised as favorite court child in the pantheon of surfing legends, these days he mixes easily with celebrity artists and Paris supermodels. Once you're accepted, however, he might christen you with another, more personalized handle. Joel loves naming things, especially his boards. He's been baiting me lately with "Pooch," but I refuse to rise to it.

"You want some of this, Chief. . . ."

Joel Tudor: slicked-back blond thatch, skinny no-bulge build, all torso. Hynsonesque in profile, a young spine married to an old face. A continuum of the cool, detached style of California surfing dating back to Kivlin and Dora. Able to divinely cross-step Malibu to charge large Pipe with uncanny positioning and grace. Took third at the Tavarua tube contest. More pro career wins than Slater. A child savant. A little bastard. A sly, smart-ass grin—and a penchant for pissing people off. An artist. A living link to surfing's past, simultaneously pointing the way to the future. Tom Morey told me: "He is reincarnation of all bitchin' stuff I love and worried God had forgotten. He surfs like we'd slave to."

Sam George recreated the venerable SURFER travel dream, this time in India's unsurfed Andaman Islands.

Volume 39 | *Number 11*

QUEST FOR FIRE

BY SAM GEORGE

MAY 18, 1998—ANDAMAN SEA

Another dawn at sea: a hot foundry, glowing from beyond the eastern horizon, its unseen fire flickering against a curtain of purple night and bright silver stars. The deck where I lie is wet with dew, and my towel blanket is soggy, but it occurs to me, before I have to get up, before another long day of inactivity begins—before I have to prove again that real love means patience, that the voyage is the destination, that if you're bored you're boring—that finding oneself curled up here on the deck of a sailboat cruising through the Andaman Sea at sunrise is a fine place to be. I'm just drifting back to sleep when suddenly there's a hand on my shoulder, a whisper. It's Chris.

"Sam, get up. There's waves."

Our first landfall. An island, one of hundreds, a shoreline, an arbitrary point on the chart, no different than any other. Promising, perhaps, due to some dispassionate markings in fathoms and shoal.

"The scene was one of striking beauty," wrote naturalist C. Boden Kloss, upon first hoving-to off these waters in 1901. "Against a background of bright blue sky, the little island rose from the sea of lapis lazuli, which ceaselessly dashed white breakers on the rocky shores."

Chris, having developed what I later deemed "left eye" on numerous Indonesian boat trips, stands on the bowsprit and points his right arm, as if steering the ship.

"There's a rideable left there," he announces.

We creep toward the sleeping island and circle, looking for a place to anchor in what turns out to be a shallow bay. The shore is a tawny slice of sand, pressed closely by a wall of foliage: hardwoods and pandunas, banks of hibiscus, vines and creepers running rampant ("like travel-

ing back to the earliest beginnings of the world," Conrad put it, taking us upriver in *Heart of Darkness*, ". . . when vegetation rioted on earth and the big trees were king").

To the north, the shoreline curves out, sand swallowed up by ferns and shallow-rooted palms, and an exposed black reef extending into the mirror-smooth blue sea. Everything is still— not a ripple, not a breath of wind. Then, flapping purposely from a branch high in a gray-trunked padouk, a white-bellied sea eagle takes wing, beating up out of the forest shadow into the sunlight. As we watch, shielding our eyes with hands, we hear a splash: Chris has quietly pulled out his board, jumped off the Crescent and is paddling across the glassy water toward the reef. I am next, racing aft to grab my board and bail, stroking quickly to catch up. We see no waves but paddle hard, like we're caught inside.

And . . . suddenly, there's this shadow, as if the sun is shining from beneath the water outside the bend of the exposed reef, casting contrast. The shadow steepens, takes shape, rolls onto itself: a wave, a left, 6 feet on the face, silver curl pitching out and folding toward a smoothly tapered shoulder. A perfect surfing wave, here, at the first spot we'd come to, before we'd even dropped anchor. And here are Chris and I alone in the lineup, watching the first peel past, the second wave in the set humping up in the exact same spot. We can only sit up and grin at each other as a third wave hits the reef in flawless symmetry. Like the Jarawa tribe whose island this is, we can't make our fire—we have to discover it.

Faint hooting from the distant ship—the lineup will be full in a minute or two. But for now, it is ours. Chris find his voice first.

"Well . . . " he says.

KELLY SLATER
TAVARUA TUBE-TIME AT SURFING'S FIRST RESORT
PHOTO: TOM SERVAIS

Aussie editor Tim Baker plumbed the dark side of the dream in Indonesia's Mentawai Islands.

Volume 39 | *Number 11*

THE SINKING ISLANDS

BY TIM BAKER

And I'd start to think, well, what's the harm? Progress is inevitable, isn't it? A few husband-and-wife teams make a good living steering their magnificent vessels around this surfing wonderland. The surfing skippers clock up untold barrels while running their stoked passengers about. A few Indonesian deckhands earn a handy income in these desperate economic times. Scores of stressed-out Western surfers swallowed up by careers rediscover their surfing stoke. The local people pick up some extra rupia selling fish or souvenirs to the tourists. Limit the number of boats, resist the construction of land camps, and protect the interests of the local communities. Put in place some strict environmental and cultural guidelines. It could all be such a good, good thing. Only human greed stands in the way.

Bush walkers treat their most treasured retreats with a holy reverence, shitting into plastic bags and carrying it out with them in their backpacks. In the Mentawais, I've seen skippers and surfers tossing beer cans overboard. I've seen bags of rubbish ferried into the islands and piles of our Western waste burned in the jungle. I've seen our own turds drifting through the lineup, the foamy discharge from the boats besmirching an entire bay. Perhaps we don't deserve the Mentawais.

How morally bankrupt are we prepared to become in our pursuit of a few perfect waves? In a country on the brink of civil war and economic collapse, where millions of people struggle just to feed themselves, and the most basic daily needs like rice and cooking oil are rendered out of reach by the suspect machinations of the world monetary system, where soldiers open fire on unarmed student demonstrators, amid all this chaos and human suffering, we surfers bicker and argue over who can wrangle a tenuous claim over which waves, curse the appearance of another boat at "our" surf spot, spuriously claiming ourselves locals by virtue of a few hours' prior occupancy. We gorge on beer and the area's thinning fish and lobster stocks, cursing local traders for trying to wrangle the best price they can out of us. We introduce the young, impressionable, local boat crews to our decadent ways and complain about corruption because the harbormaster or port officials manage to squeeze some petty cash out of us for use of these waters.

These islands are sinking, drooping in the middle from their fragile, coral rims like pies that didn't rise, swampy and boggy and rife with malaria. Palm trees topple over on the shore or sit stranded on the beaches, evidence of the shrinking islands. The besieged rain-forest tribes retreat ever inland to escape loggers, missionaries, the cancerous fungi of civilized contact. And no amount of eloquent rhapsodies about surfing's spiritual richness and brotherly, cross-cultural goodwill will convince them otherwise.

Imagine for a moment if it could somehow be different here, if surfing could be the Mentawais' salvation instead of its ruination. If every surfer who dipped a toe in these waters was obliged to contribute something to the local economy. Imagine jungle schools or medical centers funded by surfers. Imagine the Indonesian government awakened to the preciousness of the islands and its people and culture by the representations of concerned surfers. Imagine the rain forests and their incredible people protected by our raising of consciousness.

Is it just possible that surfing might enhance a place rather than corrupt it?

Traditionally, we surfers have sought out places of exceptional natural beauty and energy and gorged on them, sapped them almost dry and opened up the circumstances for their ongoing exploitation and gradual demise. Perhaps the Mentawais will be where we learn to give, to put back, to help nurture and rekindle the area's life force and natural energy.

Faced with ferocious waves almost beyond imagination, this Tahitian surf contest left its competitors—and SURFER readers—mesmerized.

Volume 40 | Number 10

RESURRECTION ALLEY

BY DEREK HYND

Cory Lopez's entry at 7:17 a.m. is stunning for its bravado. He strokes into two waves that are among the heaviest in ASP history. Two murderous assaults on the apex section. Magnitude of commitment: 10.0. Magnitude of crucifixion: 10.0. And still he keeps on ticking. Perhaps even more so than in his great Pipe effort against Derek Ho, this losing massacre will be remembered. Shane Powell lifted to take the heat with two total spitouts.

Never in the history of sport have winning pros been so penalized. The 16 heat winners from Round One move directly to Round Three and, thus, are unable to ride the second round's field of extreme dreams. Yesterday's losers become today's lucky winners—if they can handle the stress of another desperate day of very heavy water.

Ratings leader Taj Burrow, however, isn't feeling quite so lucky in his heat. Drawn against young Drollet (who, incidentally, is rated by the ASP's resident tube doyen Pierre Tostee as one of the planet's top five tubesters), Taj looks in dire straits without a wave ridden in the opening 10 minutes. Circumstances require a 20-minute man-on-man charge in nearly unrideable conditions. Taj tears into it, but Drollet is literally at home amid the beast, winning by four points. "It is simple for me," Drollet later says with the humble smile of an untouched islander. "I know which waves to catch. I know where I must be for the different swell directions. The tube? It is not so hard to find the right spot if you know the reef for the takeoff."

The loser round heat is filled with highlights. Bruce Irons again flies through the air in tongue-swallowing wipeouts, then displays casual mastery in death pits. Mick Campbell and Guiherme Herdy take wild back-to-back wipeouts. Richie Lovett rides one of the waves of his life against Wills, only to cop one of the worst head and back scrapings ever seen in pro competition (on the end section, 5 meters from the judges). O'Connell pulls back, then takes a horrific free-fall rocket to the reef. Victor Ribas, in an act of redemption after his 0.00-point Pipeline effort, worries Occy in a good heat—plenty of late drops into the barrel. But Occy is just warming up, like a lumbering human bagpipe. Nathan Fletcher toys with the foam ball against an out-of-sorts Prestage. Machado overcomes Curran in a classic tube-hunters bout that features a ton of style. Hitchings, in one of the most devastating pig-dog efforts of all time (up there with Tony Moniz and Shaun Tomson at Pipeline) against Ross Williams, logs the top scores for the round.

The dusk is full of rewind tales, too. None so vivid as Mick Lowe. Drawn once more against Andy the next day, with the forecast still strong, he dryly laments to Campbell and Occy: "Orr, it's just gonna be a life-and-death heat. Andy'll go a 9.0; I'll go a 9.5; he'll go a 10.0, and then, you know, that's when we'll really start goin' hard. One of us is gonna die."

Occy was thus reminded to call his wife, Bea. "I called her last night. I'm gonna call her again with the same concern. I want her to know I love her and that there's a chance someone's gonna die." And off he trotted.

SURFER's 1999 "Century of Surfing" issue featured this passionate—if a bit too comprehensive—overview from contributing editor Sam George.

Volume 40 | Number 10

WHEN WE WERE KINGS

BY SAM GEORGE

And it was there, being so simply a surfer, that a bright, crystalline thought occurred to me: that after all this time, after almost 100 years of swells and waves big and small, of Jack London and George Freeth and Alexander Hume Ford and the Outrigger and He'Nalu clubs; *THE DUKE AND HIS MIGHTY RIDE FROM CASTLES AND TOM BLAKE AND HIS HOLLOW BOARDS AND LORRIN HARRISON ON THE LURLINE*; of sliding along Corona del Mar jetty and camping at San Onofre and Doc Ball's California Surfriders; *OF PETE PETERSON AND PEANUTS LARSON, PADDLEBOARD COVE AND LONG BEACH FLOOD CONTROL*; of Rabbit Kekai and Don James and redwood and balsa and "sliding ass"; *OF WALLY FROISETH, WOODY BROWN, FRAN HEATH AND THE HOT CURL*; of World War II and the long, empty rights at Malibu; *OF THE STYLINGS OF JOE QUIGG, AGGIE QUIGG, MATT KIVLIN, LES WILLIAMS AND TOMMY ZAHN*; of fiberglass, polyester resin and Bob Simmons; *OF GEORGE DOWNING AND BIG WAVES, GREG NOLL, MIKE BRIGHT AND TOMMY ZAHN DOWN UNDER, CONRAD CUNHA AND WAIKIKI*; of Waimea Bay, Steamer Lane, Sunset Beach, Ventura overhead; *OF GIDGET AND MOONDOGGIE AND MICKEY DORA AND MICKEY MUÑOZ*; of Velzy, Hobie, Grubby, Sweet, Ole, Con, Hap, Bing, Wardy and Dewey; *OF "MISERLOU" AND "LET'S GO TRIPPIN'" AND "SURFIN' USA," PEROXIDE AND*

PENDLETONS, WOODIES AND BAGGIES; OF MAKAHA POINT AND ELE-PHANT GUNS; Flippy and Grigg, Van Dyke and Trent, Cole and Curren; *OF LITTLE LINDA BENSON AND THE CALHOUN GIRLS, JOHN SEVERSON'S THE SURFER AND BRUCE BROWN'S ENDLESS SUMMERS*; of Phil Edwards and his model, Murph the Surf and his jewels, Catri and his balls; *OF DONALD TAKAYAMA AND KEALOHA KAIO, OF COPPER AND CARSON, FAIN, DOYLE, CORKY, DAVID, SKIP*; Nat and Midget; Propper and Morey and Pope; *OF JOYCE HOFFMAN AND JOEY HAMASAKI, PENETRATORS AND PIPELINERS, ELIMINATORS AND EQUALIZERS, LIGHTWEIGHTS AND UFOs AND 442s AND MINI MODELS*; of Vee-bottoms and miniguns and Dick Brewer and Maui and George Greenough and Bob McTavish; *OF PINTAILS AND ACID SPLASH, JOCK AND JEFF AND JOEY CABELL*; of Waves of Change and Pacific Vibrations, the Duke Invitational, down rails and the draft; *OF WUNDERKIND LIKE MARGO, ROLF AND WAYNE*; of short johns, long johns, beavertails, honeycomb, twin-fins WAVE sets, Wax Research and Waterskates; *OF LOCALS AND LEASHES AND VW VANS, MEXICO AND MOROCCO*; of Gerry Lopez at Pipeline and John Van Ornum at the Point, Peterson and Naughton and wingers and prayers; *OF PUKA SHELLS AND AIRBRUSHED VANS AND BEACHCOMBER BILLS*; of *Huge Mondays* and *Five Summer Stories*, *Goin' Surfin* and the *Forgotten Island of Santosha*; *OF EXPRESSION SESSIONS AT ROCKY RIGHTS AND WEST PEAKS AT SUNSET, HAWKS AND OWLS, B.K., SURF MUSCLE AND HAWAIIAN RUBBERMAN*; of New-Wave Aussies like Fitzy, Kanga, P.T., Mugsy, Bugs and M.R.; *FREE RIDE BARRELS AND PIPELINE BACK-SIDE WITH THE TOMSON COUSINS AND HOT V-LAND WITH BUTTONS, LIDDEL AND DANE*; of pro tours and Pipeline Masters, Uluwatu and G-Land; *NO-NOSES AND THRUSTERS, BOOGIE BOARDS AND TIGHT TRUNKS, CHEYNE HORAN AND TOM CARROLL, MARTIN POTTER AND KONG, OCCY AND CURREN*; of Day-Glo rash guyards and modern longboards, of wave pools in Pennsylvania and surf camps in Fiji; *OF FANTASY VIDEOS, TITANIUM WETSUITS AND TINY BOARDS*; surfing granddads and the New School, Momentum and *The Endless Summer II*, more longboards and tow-ins and aerials, Jaws and Maverick's, Kelly and Occy and Kelly and Kelly and Kelly and El Niño and then Kelly again…and after all this, after all that has happened in the last 100 years, that I was still able to live a surfing life most elemental, not through some nostalgic yearning but actually experiencing in raw form the underlying current—the soul—that has run through the heart of every decade like a pulse, makes me see no reason why being a surfer in this next century will be any less fulfilling than having been one during the last.

You only have to understand the true nature of surfing, that's all.

A classic, millennium-ending surf trip to Indonesia with six-time world champion Kelly Slater, the decade's most progressive and influential surfer.

Volume 41 | Number 3

TOMORROWLAND

BY CHRIS MAURO

Watching Kelly Slater glide back into the lineup after nabbing just the third wave of his trip, I take special note of the look on his face. It's a relaxed, no-big-deal demeanor at first glance, but having witnessed the incredible ride at close range, well . . . I know better. That thing had to mean something.

Sitting perfectly still a few yards away, I aim a vicious stare at him out of the corner of my eyes. I promise myself I won't blink until he feels the heat of my glare on the side of his head. He spots the boil that's serving as his lineup spot, paddles past me, sits up on his board and begins scanning the horizon. Still, not a word.

A few seconds of eerie silence pass. Now behind him, I flick tiny droplets of water in his direction. He senses something and turns his head my way to find my interrogative stare still locked on him, demanding some kind of reaction. I know he knows what I'm waiting for, but he's still struggling to keep his cool. Finally, a huge smile crosses his face—his emotion can no longer be contained. With the guilty look of an ecstatic six-year-old who's awakened the family too early on Christmas morning, he confesses as he laughs, "Holy shit . . . that was the best wave I've caught in three years."

KELLY SLATER
FINDS THERE ARE NO LIMITS
PHOTO: ART BREWER

INDEX